Praying Your Way to a Worry-Free Life

Donna K. Maltese

Praying Your Way to a Worry-Free Life

200
Inspiring Prayers for a
Woman's Heart

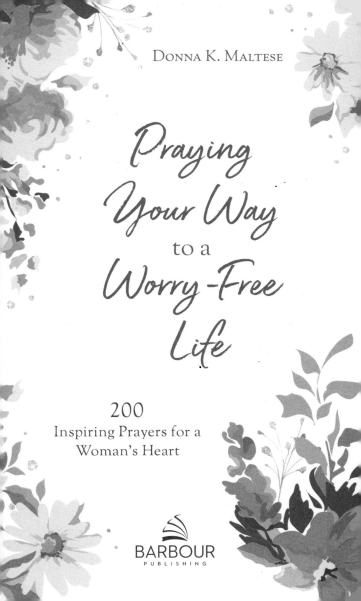

BARBOUR
PUBLISHING

Print ISBN 978-1-64352-911-0

Published by Barbour Publishing, Inc., 1810 Barbour Drive, Uhrichsville, Ohio 44683, www.barbourbooks.com

Our mission is to inspire the world with the life-changing message of the Bible.

Printed in China.

Patterned after Christ

Pattern yourselves after me
[follow my example], as I imitate
and follow Christ (the Messiah).

1 Corinthians 11:1 ampc

Lord, I want to be like You. I want to have that calm that radiates from Your presence. I want to have that peace of mind that flows like a river, never stagnant but calmly streaming its way into the hearts of all who follow You. Show me how not to worry. Help me remember that You know how many strands of hair are on my head, that You see, that You know what I need before I need it. Help me get it through my head that no matter how hard the earth shakes or how often mountains fall into the sea, You will be watching over me, keeping me safe. Remind me, Lord, that with You in my life, I can walk tall because I will lack nothing. Help me to rest secure, knowing that even when I fall asleep, You will remain with me, guarding my thoughts, holding me close, and reassuring me when I'm frightened. Help me become so secure in You that I too can walk on water and move mountains. In Your name I pray, amen.

Like a Little Child

*Truly I say to you, unless you repent (change, turn about)
and become like little children [trusting, lowly, loving,
forgiving], you can never enter the kingdom of heaven
[at all]. Whoever will humble himself therefore and
become like this little child [trusting, lowly, loving,
forgiving] is greatest in the kingdom of heaven.*

Matthew 18:3–4 AMPC

Help me, Lord, to become more like a little child. For I
know that when I trust in You, depending on You for every
need and desire, my worries will wane.

So keep me as humble, simple, modest, meek, and
forgiving as a child, Lord. Make me a more accepting
and curious person, one who looks for and expects only
the good in all things and all people. Lastly, Lord, lift me
up into Your arms when I come running to You with all
my troubles, worries, woes, and tears, looking to You for
solace, affection, and answers to all my why questions.

I ask all these things knowing that when I become
more like that little child You created me to be—more
trusting, loving, and forgiving—the closer I will be to
Your kingdom in heaven. In Jesus' name I pray, amen.

FUNDAMENTAL FACT OF FAITH

*The fundamental fact of existence is that this
trust in God, this faith, is the firm foundation under
everything that makes life worth living. It's our handle
on what we can't see. The act of faith is what distinguished
our ancestors, set them above the crowd. By faith,
we see the world called into existence by God's word,
what we see created by what we don't see.*

HEBREWS 11:1–3 MSG

Lord, You are the One who makes my life worth living.
For You give me the hope I crave and the provision I need.
This faith I have in You is my foundation, the rock that
helps me weather the storms that come my way.

My faith is the same faith that helped those who've
gone before, ones who courageously traveled into unknown territories, knowing You would be with them, help
them, guide them every step of the way.

May that same faith help me see there is more beyond
my mortal vision. For You have created and continually
will create the visible out of the invisible. And with that
power at Your command, I need not fear nor fret nor worry
about anything. That's the fundamental fact of faith. In
Jesus' name, amen.

GOD WITH US

Gideon was threshing wheat in the wine vat in order to hide it from the Midianites. Then the Angel of the LORD appeared to him and said: "The LORD is with you, mighty warrior." . . . "Go in the strength you have and deliver Israel from the power of Midian. Am I not sending you?" [Gideon] said to Him, "Please, Lord, how can I deliver Israel? Look, my family is the weakest in Manasseh, and I am the youngest in my father's house." "But I will be with you," the LORD said to him.

JUDGES 6:11–12, 14–16 HCSB

Sometimes, Lord, I feel like Gideon, hiding from the challenges that come up against me. Yet You don't see me as a weak woman from the least of families. You see me as a wonder woman of strength, power, and hope. A woman who can do what You call her to do, time after time.

Help me see me as *You* see me, Lord. Remind me that with You reigning in my life and walking by my side, I can do anything You want me to do. All I need to do is go in the strength I have—and You will do the rest. In Jesus' name, amen.

Stayed on God

*You will guard him and keep him in perfect and
constant peace whose mind [both its inclination and
its character] is stayed on You, because he commits
himself to You, leans on You, and hopes confidently
in You. So trust in the Lord (commit yourself to Him,
lean on Him, hope confidently in Him) forever; for the
Lord God is an everlasting Rock [the Rock of Ages].*

Isaiah 26:3–4 ampc

I know I'm in trouble, Lord, when my thoughts ricochet
around in my head, jumping from fretfulness to fear and
back again. Help me rein in my thoughts, Lord. Help
me focus all my faculties on You, Your love, Your power,
Your joy, Your peace. Help me to commit myself to You,
knowing You are the steady and everlasting Rock on
which I can rely. Show me how to lean on You and hope
in You, confidently knowing You are the One I can trust to
guide me in the right direction. You are the Good Shepherd who can and will care for me when I need strength,
support, comfort, protection, and provision. In Jesus'
name I live, and breathe, and pray, amen.

A Safe Place

*God is a safe place to hide, ready to help when we
need him. We stand fearless at the cliff-edge of doom,
courageous in seastorm and earthquake, before the rush
and roar of oceans, the tremors that shift mountains.
Jacob-wrestling God fights for us, GOD-of-Angel-Armies
protects us. River fountains splash joy, cooling God's city,
this sacred haunt of the Most High. God lives here, the
streets are safe, God at your service from crack of dawn.*

PSALM 46:1–5 MSG

Lord, when I am at my wits' end—which happens more
than I care to admit—I remember You. For You are my
rock and refuge, my place of safety when my entire world
feels like it is falling apart. You are the One in whom I
can hide until the storm passes or until I have the energy,
wisdom, strength, and provision to face the storm I am in.

No matter what happens, even if the earth starts to
quake and the mountains start falling into the sea, You
will hide me in Your presence, be the hedge of protection
I need no matter how big the problem or how strong the
wind. For this and so much more, I thank You. Amen.

Let Be and Be Still

*The Lord of hosts is with us; the God of Jacob is our Refuge
(our Fortress and High Tower). Selah [pause, and calmly
think of that]! . . . Let be and be still, and know (recognize
and understand) that I am God. I will be exalted among
the nations! I will be exalted in the earth! The Lord of hosts
is with us; the God of Jacob is our Refuge (our High Tower
and Stronghold). Selah [pause, and calmly think of that]!*

Psalm 46:7, 10–11 ampc

What I need in this moment is calm, Lord. Help me to get
there, to go from panicked to peace-filled. As I rest with
You in this moment, my body still and my mouth silent
before You, help my fretful thoughts to flow gently out of
my mind as I fill that newly emptied space with Your peace
and promises. Help me, King of calm, to be as still as the
surface of a pond on a windless morning. Help me to let
all things be. Help me to know, recognize, and understand
that You alone are God of all things, people, and places.
You are my refuge, high tower, and stronghold. Together
we are one in love, in peace, and in stillness. Amen.

PLEASING GOD

*By an act of faith, Enoch skipped death completely.
"They looked all over and couldn't find him because
God had taken him." We know on the basis of reliable
testimony that before he was taken "he pleased God."
It's impossible to please God apart from faith. And why?
Because anyone who wants to approach God must
believe both that he exists and that he cares enough
to respond to those who seek him.*

HEBREWS 11:5–6 MSG

I want to be so full of faith, to have so much trust in You, Lord, that I please You. But to do that, to be able to approach You, I must believe not just that You exist but that You will respond to me when I come to You with my worries, my woes, and my whys.

So here I am, Lord, standing before You. Fill me with undying faith in You. Remind me that You alone can save me from a life of worries and woes. You alone are able to help me find my way through this life. And You alone save me from myself and bring me to the place of peace I crave. In Jesus' name, amen.

The Good and Gentle Shepherd

The Lord is my Shepherd [to feed, guide,
and shield me], I shall not lack. He makes
me lie down in [fresh, tender] green pastures;
He leads me beside the still and restful waters.
He refreshes and restores my life (my self); He leads
me in the paths of righteousness [uprightness
and right standing with Him—not for my
earning it, but] for His name's sake.

PSALM 23:1–3 AMPC

As this day begins, Lord, I thank You for being my good and gentle Shepherd, the One who feeds, guides, and shields me. Because I have You in my life, working Your will in Your way, I know I will never lack.

When I need rest, You make me lie down in a comfortable place. When I need refreshment, You lead me beside still and restful waters. You restore me to myself. Lead me, Lord, by the right path—not for my own sake but for Your glory. For my aim is to please You and rest in Your peace both day and night. In Jesus' name, amen.

NOTHING IMPOSSIBLE

Then the disciples came to Jesus and asked privately,
Why could we not drive it out? He said to them, Because
of the littleness of your faith [that is, your lack of firmly
relying trust]. For truly I say to you, if you have faith [that
is living] like a grain of mustard seed, you can say to this
mountain, Move from here to yonder place, and it will
move; and nothing will be impossible to you.
MATTHEW 17:19–20 AMPC

Lord, I've been letting worries overtake me, allowing them to crowd out my knowledge of and faith in You. Help me to get back on track. To really focus on who You are and what You've already done in my life.

Revitalize my faith, Lord. Give it life so that I can confidently say to a mountain of an obstacle, "Move from here to there"—and it will move. Help me to live in line with Your will and way so that nothing will be impossible to me. For with that kind of faith in and obedience to You, my worries will wane and my faith fill out as I follow in Your footsteps. Amen.

GOD ALONE

*The armies of the Moabites, Ammonites, and some
of the Meunites declared war on Jehoshaphat. . . .
Jehoshaphat was terrified. . .and begged the LORD for
guidance. He also ordered everyone in Judah to begin
fasting. . . . He prayed, "O LORD, God of our ancestors,
you alone are the God who is in heaven. You are ruler
of all the kingdoms of the earth. You are powerful
and mighty; no one can stand against you!"*

2 CHRONICLES 20:1, 3, 6 NLT

When I hear bad news, Lord, when my future looks more
than bleak, help me to keep calm and to come to You
for guidance. Remind me who You are and what You
have done for Your people since the beginning of time.
Lead me to pray for the peace and strength I need to
meet every challenge. For You alone are the One who
reigns in heaven and on earth. You are infinitely more
powerful than any other being. No one—no man, no
woman, no king, no queen, no entity—can stand against
You. So I come to You for calm and clarity. Speak, Lord.
Speak. Amen.

EYES ON GOD

If evil comes upon us. . .we will stand before this house and before You—for Your Name [and the symbol of Your presence] is in this house—and cry to You in our affliction, and You will hear and save. . . . We have no might to stand against this great company that is coming against us. We do not know what to do, but our eyes are upon You.

2 CHRONICLES 20:9, 12 AMPC

When trouble is brewing, Lord, and I don't know what to say or think or do, I will come to You. To You I will cry for help. To You I will lift my voice. For I know that You will hear my prayer and attend to my petition. I am confident that against all odds, You will save me.

Lord, I know very well that I have no strength to stand against the trouble brought about by the evil intentions of others, but I also know that nothing can conquer You. I don't know what to do, but my eyes are fixed on You. Amen.

STAND STILL AND SEE

Be not afraid or dismayed at this great multitude;
for the battle is not yours, but God's. Tomorrow go down
to them. . . . You shall not need to fight in this battle; take
your positions, stand still, and see the deliverance of the
Lord [Who is] with you. . . . Fear not nor be dismayed.
Tomorrow go out against them, for the Lord is with you.
2 Chronicles 20:15–17 ampc

When trouble is at my door, Lord, remind me that I am not to fear or to be stunned by what I see coming against me. Instead, remind me that the battle is not mine but Yours. And all I need to do is to follow You, to go where You would have me go, to do what You would have me do.

Because You are with me, I will stand firm, still, never wavering, and watch You in action. I will not worry or be upset. Instead, I will go out and stand, knowing that You—the Lord of lords, the King of kings, whose "power no foe can withstand" (Psalm 91:1 ampc)—stand with me. In Jesus' name, amen.

17

The Power of Praise!

*Jehoshaphat stood and said, . . . Believe in the Lord
your God and you shall be established; believe and
remain steadfast to His prophets and you shall prosper.
When he had consulted with the people, he appointed
singers to sing to the Lord and praise Him in their holy
[priestly] garments as they went out before the army,
saying, Give thanks to the Lord, for His mercy
and loving-kindness endure forever!*

2 Chronicles 20:20–21 ampc

I can't imagine it, Lord, but it's true. A king sent praise singers out in front of his warriors to fend off three armies. And because the king and his people believed in You, You gave them victory—and what a victory it was!

So help me, Lord, to do more praising than praying. Show me how praise carries more power than a fully equipped fighting force—or anything else that may come against me.

You have a knack, Lord, for making those who seem helpless the victors because they trust in You, Your promises, and Your Word. Give me that kind of faith, Lord, so that I too can stand strong no matter who or what comes my way. In Jesus' name, amen.

VALLEY OF BLESSINGS

*When they began to sing and to praise, the Lord set
ambushments against the men of Ammon, Moab, and
Mount Seir. . . . They all helped to destroy one another. . . .
Jehoshaphat and his people. . .were three days in gathering
the spoil. On the fourth day they assembled in the Valley of
Beracah. There they blessed the Lord. So the name of the
place is still called the Valley of Beracah [blessing].*
2 Chronicles 20:22–23, 25–26 ampc

When my worries and troubles are getting me down, Lord,
remind me of the way You handled the armies against
Your people. How You fought for people and how their
praises to You ended up being their most powerful weapon
against their foes. And not only did You bring them an
amazing victory, but You gifted them with so much spoil
it took them three days to gather it all up! You are more
than a wonder-worker, more than a refuge and stronghold.
You are the Lord of miracles and the God of blessings
to whom I lift my voice in praise. Amen.

By Faith

By faith, Noah built a ship in the middle of dry land.
He was warned about something he couldn't see, and acted
on what he was told. The result? His family was saved.
His act of faith drew a sharp line between the evil of the
unbelieving world and the rightness of the believing world.
As a result, Noah became intimate with God.

HEBREWS 11:7 MSG

Lord, I can imagine all the ribbing Noah got as he followed Your command to build an enormous boat and, to complicate matters, did so "in the middle of dry land"! All because You warned him of what was coming, something he could not yet see or hear. He acted only on what You told him. And because of his faith in You and his willingness to obey no matter how much he was mocked, he not only was able to save his family—as well as the future of humankind and animal-kind—but became even closer to You! So many blessings rolled into one act of extreme faith in extreme times. Help me to be a Noah, Lord—to follow You and Your commands no matter how it looks in the eyes of an unbelieving world. In Jesus' name, amen.

In Step with God

Yes, though I walk through the [deep, sunless] valley of the shadow of death, I will fear or dread no evil, for You are with me; Your rod [to protect] and Your staff [to guide], they comfort me. You prepare a table before me in the presence of my enemies. You anoint my head with oil; my [brimming] cup runs over. Surely or only goodness, mercy, and unfailing love shall follow me all the days of my life, and through the length of my days the house of the Lord [and His presence] shall be my dwelling place.

PSALM 23:4–6 AMPC

In step with You, Lord, I know I need not fear or dread anything. Because You are with me. You use Your rod to protect me and Your staff to guide me. I need no other reassurance than that, for You are my Comforter. With You on my side, my enemies are powerless to hurt me or steal my peace. You have anointed me with Your Spirit, and I know that only goodness, mercy, and love will follow me all my life as I dwell in You. Amen.

THE EXTRA MILE

*"If anyone slaps you on the right cheek, turn to
him the other also. And if anyone would sue you
and take your tunic, let him have your cloak as well.
And if anyone forces you to go one mile, go with
him two miles. Give to the one who begs from you,
and do not refuse the one who would borrow from you."*

Matthew 5:39–42 esv

Some things that I might worry about, Lord, are things
You want me to allow to happen. If someone hurts me,
I'm to remain vulnerable and allow her to injure me again.
If anyone takes my shirt, I'm to give my coat. If someone forces me to walk one mile with her, I'm to go an
extra mile as well. And I'm to give to the one who begs,
while allowing another to borrow. All of those things
seem to go against what might give me peace. Yet that's
how You work, wanting us to live by our spirit, not by our
flesh. If that's what You want, I'm up for living that way,
Lord, as long as You stay by my side. For with You beside
me on this journey, I know all will be well. Amen.

By an Act of Faith

*By an act of faith, Abraham said yes to God's call
to travel to an unknown place that would become his
home. When he left he had no idea where he was going.
By an act of faith he lived in the country promised him,
lived as a stranger camping in tents. Isaac and Jacob
did the same, living under the same promise.*

Hebrews 11:8–9 msg

I can't imagine packing up my family and household goods, leaving my home, and going on a trip to a place I've never seen before. Heading out without a map, just waiting for You to say, "Stop here. This is the place." Yet that's what You called Abraham to do. And that's what You call me to do. To go where no woman has gone before, walking Your way, according to Your promise and timeline. That takes a leap of faith. Yet I know You are a God who keeps His word. So here I am, Lord. Tell me where You would have me go. And as I follow in faith, give me peace for the journey. In Jesus' name, amen.

Under His Wings

Those who live in the shelter of the Most High will find rest in the shadow of the Almighty. This I declare about the LORD: He alone is my refuge, my place of safety; he is my God, and I trust him. For he will rescue you from every trap and protect you from deadly disease. He will cover you with his feathers. He will shelter you with his wings. His faithful promises are your armor and protection.

PSALM 91:1–4 NLT

Lead me into Your presence, Lord. Help me find rest in Your shadow. For You alone are my refuge. You are my fortress, a place where no one can touch me. You, my Lord and Savior, are my God—*the* God. In You alone I trust. For I know You will rescue me from every trap that is set against me. You will protect me from any harm headed my way. Best of all, You, like a father eagle, will cover me with Your feathers, providing me shelter, whether good weather or foul. You have surrounded me with Your presence, Your promises, and Your protection—all of which birth peace within me. Amen.

A Win-Win Situation

*Because you have made the LORD—my refuge,
the Most High—your dwelling place, no harm will
come to you; no plague will come near your tent. For He
will give His angels orders concerning you, to protect you
in all your ways. They will support you with their hands
so that you will not strike your foot against a stone.*

PSALM 91:9–12 HCSB

So many benefits come with making You my refuge, Lord. When I depend on You and trust in You, I always end up in a win-win situation. When I trust You to be my refuge, when I have the sense and faith to dwell in You, You—the one powerful God of the universe—not only promise that no harm will come to me, but also promise to order Your angels to watch over me, to protect me in every way. You have commanded them to support me with their hands so I don't trip up.

For all this and so much more, Lord, I thank You—with all my heart, all my thanks, and all my praise. Amen.

A Personal
Knowledge of God

*Because he has set his love upon Me, therefore will
I deliver him; I will set him on high, because he knows
and understands My name [has a personal knowledge of
My mercy, love, and kindness—trusts and relies on Me,
knowing I will never forsake him, no, never]. He shall call
upon Me, and I will answer him; I will be with him in
trouble, I will deliver him and honor him. With long
life will I satisfy him and show him My salvation.*

PSALM 91:14–16 AMPC

I want to know more about You, Lord. For the more I know about You, the fewer my worries and the greater my peace of mind, the fewer my frets and the greater my faith. Lead me, Lord, through Your Word. Tell me what You would have me know. Show me where You would have me go. Reveal what You would have me see. Say what You would have me hear. For as I learn more about Your faithfulness to me, I'll understand that You will never leave me. That when I call, You will answer. That when I'm in trouble, You'll deliver me. Amen.

THE WATER WALKER

*[Jesus' disciples] got into the boat and headed across
the lake toward Capernaum. Soon a gale swept down
upon them, and the sea grew very rough. They had rowed
three or four miles when suddenly they saw Jesus walking
on the water toward the boat. They were terrified, but he
called out to them, "Don't be afraid. I am here!" Then they
were eager to let him in the boat, and immediately
they arrived at their destination!*

JOHN 6:17–21 NLT

Lord of all, when I am surrounded by clouds and darkness,
when I find myself in panic mode, help me recognize the
comfort and deliverance that come with Your presence.
Help me not to react in fear. When You are looking to be
there for me, to be my Guard and Rescuer, open up my
ears and my mind to Your words, "Do not be afraid. I
am here."

For when I realize who You are, I will be eager to
let You into my boat. For I know that when You, the Great
I Am, are sailing with me, I will reach my true destination more swiftly. In Your name I pray, amen.

Nothing Too Difficult

"Ah, Lord God! It is you who have made the heavens and the earth by your great power and by your outstretched arm! Nothing is too hard for you. You show steadfast love to thousands, but you repay the guilt of fathers to their children after them, O great and mighty God, whose name is the Lord of hosts, great in counsel and mighty in deed."

Jeremiah 32:17–19 esv

Sometimes, Lord, when I'm in a difficult situation and see no way out, remind me who You are—the One who made the heavens and the earth by Your power and strength. Nothing is too difficult for You. There is no stone You cannot lift, no sea You cannot divide, no wind You cannot tame, no desert You cannot reclaim, no force You cannot defeat. You are the almighty God. At the same time, You are my gentle Shepherd, the One who loves me like no other. With You, the greatest, mightiest, and most loving God, by my side and within my heart, I know I never need to be afraid. Amen.

BELIEVING THE PROMISE

*By faith, barren Sarah was able to become pregnant,
old woman as she was at the time, because she believed the
One who made a promise would do what he said. That's
how it happened that from one man's dead and shriveled
loins there are now people numbering into the millions.*
HEBREWS 11:11–12 MSG

You are amazing, Lord. You always come through on Your
promises. You work miracles no matter how impossible
a breakthrough seems.

When You promised Sarah and Abraham a son,
Sarah actually laughed. Yet You countered with "Is anything too hard or too wonderful for the Lord?" (Genesis
18:14 AMPC). Then You promised You'd be back the next
year, at which time Sarah would be holding a son in her
arms. And Your words became her reality! At the age of
ninety, Sarah gave birth to a son, to the delight of the new
father, a one-hundred-year-old Abraham!

Lord, help me to have the faith of Abraham and
the joy of Sarah, ones who received just as You had
promised. Remind me of all the other promises You have
stood behind as I trust that Your Word always proves
true. In Jesus' name, amen.

BELOVED SHEPHERD

His banner over me was love [for love waved as a
protecting and comforting banner over my head when I
was near him]. . . . [I can feel] his left hand under my head
and his right hand embraces me! . . . [Vividly she pictured
it] The voice of my beloved [shepherd]! Behold, he comes,
leaping upon the mountains. . . . My beloved speaks and
says to me, Rise up, my love, my fair one, and come away.
SONG OF SOLOMON 2:4, 6, 8, 10 AMPC

In Your presence, Lord, I close my eyes and feel Your love
surrounding me. I can feel Your left hand cradling my head,
Your right hand pulling me close. I can feel Your breath
upon my skin, hear Your heartbeat in rhythm with mine.
Where You are is where I want to be, my Beloved. For
You are my gentle Shepherd, the One who hears when
I cry, the One who stays by my side until my fears have
waned. And when You say, "Rise up, My love, My fair one,
and come away," You know I will follow You willingly,
wherever You would have me go. For You are my beloved
Shepherd. Amen.

SOURCE OF COMFORT

Blessed be the God and Father of our Lord Jesus Christ,
the Father of sympathy (pity and mercy) and the God
[Who is the Source] of every comfort (consolation and
encouragement), Who comforts (consoles and encourages)
us in every trouble (calamity and affliction), so that we
may also be able to comfort (console and encourage) those
who are in any kind of trouble or distress, with the comfort
(consolation and encouragement) with which we ourselves
are comforted (consoled and encouraged) by God.

2 CORINTHIANS 1:3–4 AMPC

When I am weary, fearful, upset, grieving, or worried, I
look for You, Lord. For You alone can see into my heart
and mind and know what I need and long for. For You
are the Father of all mercy and the God of all comfort.
When I am troubled, I need look no further than You,
seeking Your calm, Your peace, Your encouragement,
Your understanding and comfort. Remind me, Lord, that
at some point, when my time of difficulty is over, I will
be equipped to encourage, to comfort, to listen to others
suffering from the same troubles I've already endured. In
Jesus' name, amen.

GOD ON YOUR SIDE

*Light, space, zest—that's GOD! So, with him on my
side I'm fearless, afraid of no one and nothing. When
vandal hordes ride down ready to eat me alive, those
bullies and toughs fall flat on their faces. When besieged,
I'm calm as a baby. When all hell breaks loose, I'm collected
and cool. I'm asking GOD for one thing, only one thing:
to live with him in his house my whole life long.*

PSALM 27:1–4 MSG

Sometimes, Lord, I fear that I fear too much. Thinking
about my fears takes me to a place of worry, a place where
I don't want to go and especially don't want to remain. So
here I am, digging into Your Word and taking my concerns
to You in prayer.

Lord, with You on my side, I need not fear anyone
or anything. When evil powers come against me, You will
protect me, shield me, lift me up—and their intents will
come to naught. That's why I can be as calm as a just-fed
baby, as quiet as the surface of a pond. Because You are
with me, I know all will be well. In Jesus' name, amen.

Prompted by Faith

*[Prompted] by faith Moses, after his birth, was kept
concealed for three months by his parents, because they
saw how comely the child was; and they were not overawed
and terrified by the king's decree. [Aroused] by faith Moses,
when he had grown to maturity and become great, refused
to be called the son of Pharaoh's daughter, because he
preferred to share the oppression [suffer the hardships]
and bear the shame of the people of God rather than to
have the fleeting enjoyment of a sinful life.*
Hebrews 11:23–25 AMPC

Lord, I'm amazed at some of the choices Your people made
under the worst of circumstances. I envy the faith they
had in You. Today, I claim that measure of faith for myself.

Today, I refuse to be frightened by the evil behavior
of others, people who don't know You. No matter what
statements they make or actions they take, I'm counting
on You to keep me safe and sound. Then, in that calm
place, I know my faith will lead me where You want me to
go. And no matter how arduous the journey, all that will
matter is that I'm taking it with You. Amen.

At His Feet

I'll contemplate his beauty; I'll study at his feet.
That's the only quiet, secure place in a noisy world,
the perfect getaway, far from the buzz of traffic.
God holds me head and shoulders above all who try
to pull me down. I'm headed for his place to offer
anthems that will raise the roof! Already I'm
singing God-songs; I'm making music to GOD.

PSALM 27:4–6 MSG

When I feel so ensconced in worry that I can't find my way out of panic and into Your peace, I want to come to You, Lord. I'm going to sit at Your feet, rest my head against Your knees, and soak in Your Word. It is there I will find the peace I yearn for, the calm I crave. There I will find the wisdom I need to change up my thoughts and get my head straight. Caught up in Your presence, I know You'll lift me up, way above those who are trying to drag me down to their levels. Instead of going their way, I'm heading Your way, Lord, finding the higher road, the better way of living, breathing, and being in You. All praise to the God of peace! Amen.

Motivated by Faith

[Motivated] by faith he left Egypt behind him,
being unawed and undismayed by the wrath of the king;
for he never flinched but held staunchly to his purpose
and endured steadfastly as one who gazed on Him
Who is invisible. By faith (simple trust and confidence in
God) he instituted and carried out the Passover and the
sprinkling of the blood [on the doorposts], so that the
destroyer of the firstborn (the angel) might not
touch those [of the children of Israel].
Hebrews 11:27–28 ampc

Make me more like Moses, Lord. Although he had times when he lacked confidence in himself, he never lacked confidence in You. That's how he was able to stay on the right pathway, not allowing anyone—no matter how powerful or evil—to keep him from doing what You called him to do.

Even though I can't see You with my physical eyes, I have faith in Your presence, power, and purpose. For I seek Your Spirit within me, knowing that with You in my heart, mind, and soul, I can do anything You call me to do. You alone are my motivation to live this life for You. In Jesus' name, amen.

An Outstretched Arm

*You brought forth Your people Israel out of the
land of Egypt with signs and wonders, with a strong
hand and outstretched arm. . .You gave them this land
which You swore to their fathers to give them, a land
flowing with milk and honey; and they entered and
took possession of it. . . . Then came the word of the
Lord to Jeremiah, saying, Behold, I am the Lord,
the God of all flesh; is there anything too hard for Me?*
JEREMIAH 32:21–23, 26–27 AMPC

Amazingly enough, Lord, *nothing* is too difficult for You.
That fact is proven by Your Word, which holds numer-
ous examples of You doing what seems impossible. You
made the sun stand still for Joshua. You turned five fish
and two loaves of bread into enough food to feed five
thousand men—not including the women and children
with them! You whisked Elijah away on a fiery chariot
that carried him up to heaven. You parted the sea, walked
on water, and calmed the waves. If You can do all that
and so much more, I know You can lead me to a place of
peace. In You. Amen.

His Hands Alone

*We do not want you to be uninformed, brethren,
about the affliction and oppressing distress which
befell us in [the province of] Asia, how we were so utterly
and unbearably weighed down and crushed that we
despaired even of life [itself]. Indeed, we felt within
ourselves that we had received the [very] sentence of death,
but that was to keep us from trusting in and depending
on ourselves instead of on God Who raises the dead.*

2 Corinthians 1:8–9 ampc

There are times, Lord, when my troubles, my worries, my circumstances bring me so low that I have only one way to go—up. To You. You are the One I have to trust when I come to the end of myself. You are the only One who can deliver me from both troubles that come against me from others and problems I may have caused myself. I find such comfort in that knowledge, Lord. Although I know *I* will falter, I know You never will. That is why I trust in and depend on You alone, putting all I have, all I am, and all I dream to be in Your hands. In Jesus' name, amen.

In the Land of the Living

Lord, hear my voice when I call; be gracious to me and answer me. . . . Show me Your way, Lord, and lead me on a level path. . . . I am certain that I will see the Lord's goodness in the land of the living. Wait for the Lord; be strong and courageous. Wait for the Lord.

Psalm 27:7, 11, 13–14 hcsb

Here I am, Lord, coming to You, resting at Your feet, waiting for the wisdom I need to see me through this day and the night that follows. I know that when I seek You, I will find You, for You care for me. You will never abandon me, lose me, or forsake me.

Lord, guide me to a smooth path, a path clearly marked out for me. Help me find the hope I've been seeking. And if I stand in a place of uncertainty, lead me to the goodness I know awaits me in the land of the living. If impatience starts to nibble at my confidence, remind me to wait for You. In the meantime, keep me strong and brave, confident Your answer is on its way. Amen.

Keep on Believing

*Jairus. . .prostrated himself at His feet and begged
Him earnestly, saying, My little daughter is at the point
of death. Come and lay Your hands on her, so that she
may be healed and live. . . . There came some from the
ruler's house, who said [to Jairus], Your daughter has
died. Why bother and distress the Teacher any further?
Overhearing but ignoring what they said, Jesus said to
the ruler of the synagogue, Do not be seized with alarm
and struck with fear; only keep on believing.*

MARK 5:22–23, 35–36 AMPC

I'm coming to You, Lord, laying myself and my worries at
Your feet. I know You can fix anything. And so I ask You
to enter into my situation, alleviate my trouble, make my
circumstances clear, and guide me where You'd have me
go. Help me to stop worrying and just leave all things
in Your hands. For no matter what I hear from fellow
humans, I know You have the final and definitive answer
for me and mine. So I will muffle the voices of assumption,
the feelings of fear, and zero in on Your voice alone, the
voice that continually tells me, "Do not fear. Only keep
on believing!"

GOOD SUCCESS

*This Book of the Law shall not depart out of your mouth,
but you shall meditate on it day and night, that you
may observe and do according to all that is written in it.
For then you shall make your way prosperous, and then
you shall deal wisely and have good success. Have not
I commanded you? Be strong, vigorous, and very
courageous. Be not afraid, neither be dismayed,
for the Lord your God is with you wherever you go.*

JOSHUA 1:8–9 AMPC

I'm passionate about Your Word, Lord. I love soaking myself in it, talking about it, thinking about it night and day. Knowing so much about You and Your way helps me to follow You, to know the path You would have me walk. For I know that when I'm following in Your footprints, I'm heading in the right direction and things will work out well. With the wisdom of Your Word in my heart, mind, and spirit, I know I can find the strength and courage I need to do what You would have me do. With You going before me, walking beside me, and watching my back, success is ours. Amen.

CHAMPION OF THE FAITHFUL

*By an act of faith, Israel walked through the Red Sea
on dry ground. The Egyptians tried it and drowned. By
faith, the Israelites marched around the walls of Jericho for
seven days, and the walls fell flat. By an act of faith, Rahab,
the Jericho harlot, welcomed the spies and escaped the
destruction that came on those who refused to trust God.*

HEBREWS 11:29–31 MSG

The wonders You've performed so that Your faithful could
go where You told them to go are stupendous. But each
of those wonders was performed only *after* Your people
did what You commanded them to do—no matter how
strange, questionable, or unreasonable they thought Your
directions were at the time! When Your people seemed
to be stuck between the Egyptians and the Red Sea and
all seemed lost, You parted the sea. You brought down
the walls of Jericho after Your people spent seven days
marching around them. And You used a woman of ill
repute to help Your spies—and that same woman and
her family—escape destruction. That is why all my hope
and trust lie in You, the Champion of the faithful. Amen.

From Mountains to Molehills

For who are you, O great mountain [of human obstacles]?
Before Zerubbabel [who with Joshua had led the return
of the exiles from Babylon and was undertaking the
rebuilding of the temple, before him] you shall become
a plain [a mere molehill]! And he shall bring forth the
finishing gable stone [of the new temple] with loud
shoutings of the people, crying, Grace, grace to it!
ZECHARIAH 4:7 AMPC

Lord, sometimes I make my challenges into giant mountains. In my mind they become almost too much to overcome. They grow into obstacles too huge to get over, under, or around. The next thing I know, I'm in a mess, not knowing what to do. Soon my feelings have taken me over. Then I remember You. I remember who You are. I hear the words of Your angel about Zerubbabel, and I recall that because I am Your daughter, You will reduce my mountain to a molehill! You will make me triumph over every obstacle! All glory and honor to You, Lord, Diminisher of mountains!

CONTINUAL SAVINGS

[For it is He] Who rescued and saved us from such
a perilous death, and He will still rescue and save us;
in and on Him we have set our hope (our joyful and
confident expectation) that He will again deliver us
[from danger and destruction and draw us to Himself],
while you also cooperate by your prayers for us
[helping and laboring together with us].

2 CORINTHIANS 1:10–11 AMPC

Lord, when I find myself moaning and groaning, chewing my nails, grinding my teeth in worry over all the crazy things going on in the world, I always come back to the fact that You have delivered me and will continue to deliver me over and over again. That's why I can remain calm in the midst of chaos. For I don't put my hope in people or in great movements. No. All my hope, all my joy, all my confidence, all my expectations are fixed on You, Lord. For people, things, and money are perishable. They and their power fade away. But You, the One who continually watches over me and cares for me, will never fade, never forsake me , never forget me. In You alone I trust. Amen.

What a Plan

"I know the plans I have for you, declares the Lord,
*plans for welfare and not for evil, to give you a future and
a hope. Then you will call upon me and come and pray
to me, and I will hear you. You will seek me and find me,
when you seek me with all your heart. I will be found by
you, declares the* Lord, *and I will restore your fortunes."*

Jeremiah 29:11–14 esv

Some days, Lord, I'm not sure if I'm in the right place
or if I've made the right decision. I look around me and
wonder where I've been, where I am, and where I might
be going. I start worrying that maybe I should be doing
something else, living somewhere else, loving someone
else. Then, when I finally quiet myself, I hear Your voice
reminding me that You have plans for me, plans for my
good, to give me hope and a future. That all I need to do
is call on You, run to You, pray to You, and You will hear
my voice. That when I seek You—with all my heart—You
will be found and my fortunes restored. What a Lord!
What a promise! What a plan!

Restored

There was a woman who had had a flow of blood for twelve years. . . . She had heard the reports concerning Jesus, and she came up behind Him in the throng and touched His garment, for she kept saying, If I only touch His garments, I shall be restored to health. And immediately her flow of blood was dried up at the source, and [suddenly] she felt in her body that she was healed of her [distressing] ailment.

Mark 5:25, 27–29 ampc

Jesus, I have a chronic issue. One I can't seem to get relief from. I feel like the woman with the issue of blood. I've heard about You. I know what You can do for Your children. I keep telling myself that if I can just touch You, reach out and connect with You heart-to-heart, I will be healed. You will say to me, "Daughter, your confidence in Me has restored you. Now go in peace." So here I am, Lord. I'm coming to You, stretching out to touch the hem of Your garment, knowing You can heal all, waiting for Your power to flow into me. . .knowing my faith in You will restore me.

My Part

I will be with you; I will not fail you or forsake you.
Be strong (confident) and of good courage, for you
shall cause this people to inherit the land which I swore
to their fathers to give them. Only you be strong and
very courageous, that you may do according to all the
law which Moses My servant commanded you.
Turn not from it to the right hand or to the left,
that you may prosper wherever you go.

JOSHUA 1:5–7 AMPC

So many times, Lord, You tell me that You are with me, will never fail nor leave me. And that my part is to be strong, to be brave, to do all You tell me to do. You tell me I should never deviate from Your Word and the path it urges me to take. You say if I do all that, I will prosper wherever I go. It sounds easy, Lord, but it's not. Sometimes You may be with me, but I move off course. I fail to see You—sometimes I even fail to look for You. Then I find myself becoming fearful and losing confidence. So, Lord, remind me every day of my part. And I'll take courage knowing Yours.

By the Help of Faith

*Time would fail me to tell of Gideon, Barak,
Samson, Jephthah, of David and Samuel and the
prophets, who by [the help of] faith subdued kingdoms,
administered justice, obtained promised blessings, closed
the mouths of lions, extinguished the power of raging fire,
escaped the devourings of the sword, out of frailty and
weakness won strength and became stalwart, even mighty
and resistless in battle, routing alien hosts.*

Hebrews 11:32–34 ampc

I'm amazed, Lord, by what You can accomplish through
Your people. Even though I'm only one person, prompted
and empowered by my faith in You, I too can obtain the
promises with which You've blessed us. I can close the
mouths of roaring predators, put out the flames of evil,
escape those who come against me, and become mighty
and invincible when fighting for Your good. With You
within me, going before me, walking beside me, and watching over, I cannot lose. Any worries that I've been
entertaining—both large and small—are vanquished
by my faith and trust in You, leaving me with only one
question. What would You have me do today in Your
name? Amen.

YOUR RESCUING KNIGHT

GOD is bedrock under my feet, the castle in which I live,
my rescuing knight. My God—the high crag where I run
for dear life, hiding behind the boulders, safe in the granite
hideout; my mountaintop refuge, he saves me from ruthless
men. I sing to GOD the Praise-Lofty, and find myself safe
and saved. . . . A hostile world! I called to GOD, to my
God I cried out. From his palace he heard me call; my cry
brought me right into his presence—a private audience!

2 SAMUEL 22:2–4, 7 MSG

Growing up, I heard a lot of fairy tales about princesses
being rescued. But that was far from my reality until I
met You. For You, Lord, are my Prince, my Knight in
shining armor. You're the rock I stand on, the castle in
which I dwell, the One I run to when I'm afraid and want
to hide. You're my fortress, the place where no one can
reach me. So to You I'll sing my praise, for You are the
real thing. When I'm in trouble and call out to You,
I know You'll not only hear me but bring me straight
into Your presence, safe and sound. What a Knight!
Amen.

Press On

I press on to possess that perfection for which Christ Jesus first possessed me. No, dear brothers and sisters, I have not achieved it, but I focus on this one thing: Forgetting the past and looking forward to what lies ahead, I press on to reach the end of the race and receive the heavenly prize for which God, through Christ Jesus, is calling us.

PHILIPPIANS 3:12–14 NLT

Lord, every time I turn back and get hung up on the past, worrying about what I could have or should have done back then, I end up stumbling on my path. So I'm coming to You for help. Help me to stop focusing on the past. Help me to forget what has gone before. I know that although I can't change the past, I can do better in the present and look forward to what lies ahead. Fill me, Lord God, with the energy, strength, power, and wisdom to press on. For my goal, my aim, is to reach the end of this journey and obtain that wonderful prize to which You, through Jesus, are calling me. In His wonderful name I pray, amen.

GOD GOES BEFORE YOU

*Be strong, courageous, and firm; fear not nor be in
terror before them, for it is the Lord your God Who goes
with you; He will not fail you or forsake you. . . . Be strong,
courageous, and firm. . . . It is the Lord Who goes before
you; He will [march] with you; He will not fail you or
let you go or forsake you; [let there be no cowardice or
flinching, but] fear not, neither become broken [in spirit—
depressed, dismayed, and unnerved with alarm].*

DEUTERONOMY 31:6–8 AMPC

Over and over again I need to hear Your words telling me
to be strong, to have courage, and to stand firm. Because,
Lord, You have promised You not only will go with me
but will never fail me. Nor will You forsake me. And at
the same time You're going before me, checking things
out before I get there, You are also marching with me!
Only You, God, can be in every place at the same time,
making sure I come to no harm. Your presence gives me
the confidence I need, the calm I crave, and the joy my
heart cries out for. Thank You, Lord, for Your empower-
ing presence and so much more. Amen.

"ALL IS WELL"

The child sat on her lap till noon, and then he died.
And she went up and laid him on the bed of the man
of God and shut the door behind him and went out. Then
she called to her husband and said, "Send me one of the
servants and one of the donkeys, that I may quickly go to
the man of God and come back again." And he said,
"Why will you go to him today? It is neither new
moon nor Sabbath." She said, "All is well."

2 KINGS 4:20–23 ESV

Lord, I want to be like this Shunammite woman, one who takes action, takes the necessary steps instead of being mired in worries. I want to be calm amid chaos, have peace amid pressure. I want to understand and know that all I really need to do during pain and heartbreak is come to You, seek Your face, Your Word, Your power, wisdom, and strength. And when people ask me questions, wondering why I'm taking the faith steps I'm taking, I want to be able to say to them, "Don't worry. All is well." And to believe it. In Jesus' name, amen.

DOING THE WORD

Don't just listen to God's word. You must do what it says.
Otherwise, you are only fooling yourselves. For if you listen
to the word and don't obey, it is like glancing at your face in
a mirror. You see yourself, walk away, and forget what you
look like. But if you look carefully into the perfect law that
sets you free, and if you do what it says and don't forget
what you heard, then God will bless you for doing it.
JAMES 1:22–25 NLT

I admit it, Lord. Sometimes I get into a slump, just half-
heartedly reading Your Word but not doing anything with
it. Then I wonder why I feel untethered or have trouble
focusing. So help me, Lord, not just to listen to what You
have to say through Your Word, but to actually do what
it says. Remind me that Your Word shows me the truth,
and that truth is what will set me free. Help me keep in
mind that when I do what You say and remember what
I've heard, You will bless me. In Jesus' name, amen.

EYES

Elisha's servant said to him, Alas, my master!
What shall we do? [Elisha] answered, Fear not;
for those with us are more than those with them.
Then Elisha prayed, Lord, I pray You, open his eyes
that he may see. And the Lord opened the young
man's eyes, and he saw, and behold, the mountain was
full of horses and chariots of fire round about Elisha.
2 KINGS 6:15–17 AMPC

I feel a bit like Elisha's servant, Lord. I'm looking around
me and seeing nothing but trouble. Next thing I know,
I can't even move for I don't know what to do or where
to go! And then I, Your servant, turn to You. I ask, "Oh,
God! What shall we do?" And You tell me not to fear—
because those with us are more than what is needed to
conquer my trouble, answer my questions, and lead me
to victory. You open my eyes so that I might see that with
You on my side, victory over all things (trouble, worry,
fear, dread, panic) is imminent. For Your host of horses
and chariots of fire is an impenetrable wall of protection
around me. Amen.

THE GREATEST TEACHER

Then we will no longer be immature like children. We won't be tossed and blown about by every wind of new teaching. We will not be influenced when people try to trick us with lies so clever they sound like the truth. Instead, we will speak the truth in love, growing in every way more and more like Christ, who is the head of his body, the church.
EPHESIANS 4:14–15 NLT

Lord, there are days when I seem to lose my footing. Some people have strange ideas of what it means to be a Christian. They teach things that don't seem to be in line with Your Word. And then they act on those teachings. Knowing how to respond to these people and their strange ideas can be confusing.

So help me, Lord, to stick with Your Word and keep to Your true way. Help me not to be like some babe in the woods who doesn't know the first thing about what it means to be a woman of Christ. Help me not to be influenced by those who are not of You. And above all, help me to speak Your truth in love. For I want to become more like Your Son, Jesus Christ, who is the greatest Teacher of all. Amen.

God's Help

Fear not [there is nothing to fear], for I am with you;
do not look around you in terror and be dismayed,
for I am your God. I will strengthen and harden you to
difficulties, yes, I will help you; yes, I will hold you up and
retain you with My [victorious] right hand of rightness and
justice. . . . For I the Lord your God hold your right hand;
I am the Lord, Who says to you, Fear not; I will help you!
ISAIAH 41:10, 13 AMPC

In these troubled times, Lord, help me not to look around me in terror but rather to look to You only. For standing with You, I have nothing to fear.

You are the God of all gods. You are the One who gives me the strength I need to bear up. You remind me of past difficulties I've had and how You got me through. You not only help me but hold me up and keep me safe. You promise to protect me from anything that comes against me. You'll keep me safe as You hold my hand and say, "Don't fear, little one. I'm here. And I'll help." Amen.

KEY TO PEACE

Always be full of joy in the Lord. I say it again—rejoice! . . .
Don't worry about anything; instead, pray about
everything. Tell God what you need, and thank him for
all he has done. Then you will experience God's peace,
which exceeds anything we can understand. His peace will
guard your hearts and minds as you live in Christ Jesus.

PHILIPPIANS 4:4, 6–7 NLT

No matter what happens, Lord, I want to be full of joy!
The joy that is found in You alone. So I'm looking to
learn from You, Lord, how not to worry. Instead, I want
to pray about anything and everything—no matter
how tremendous, how terrible, or how trivial it seems.
I want to lay all my concerns at Your feet, tell You what
I need to go forward, and thank You for everything You
have done for me. For I know that only then will I have
some idea of what Your peace is like. Only then will Your
peace become a protective barrier, guarding my heart
and mind as I live in Jesus the Christ, my Key to peace.

SAFELY CRADLED

You have freed me when I was hemmed in and
enlarged me when I was in distress; have mercy upon
me and hear my prayer. . . . You have put more joy
and rejoicing in my heart than [they know] when
their wheat and new wine have yielded abundantly.
In peace I will both lie down and sleep, for You, Lord,
alone make me dwell in safety and confident trust.

PSALM 4:1, 7–8 AMPC

You, Lord, have always answered my prayers for help. So
I call upon You now. I ask You to help me overcome a
fretful mind. You've freed me from so many traps in the
past, and I ask You to do so again.

Hear my prayer, Giver of all things. Imbue me with
the peace that surpasses all understanding. Replace my
fretting with the joy I find in You alone. Enlighten my
mind and lighten my heart. Help me trust in You alone.
For then I will have the peace I yearn for. The calm I
need in mind, body, spirit, and soul. The quiet confidence
I require so I can both lie down and sleep, cradled in
Your arms of safety. Amen.

DWELLING PLACES

Do not let your hearts be troubled (distressed, agitated).
You believe in and adhere to and trust in and rely on God;
believe in and adhere to and trust in and rely also on Me.
In My Father's house there are many dwelling places (homes).
If it were not so, I would have told you; for I am going away
to prepare a place for you. . . . I will come back again and
will take you to Myself, that where I am you may be also.

JOHN 14:1–3 AMPC

What a relief, Lord, to know that You have gone before me to prepare a special place for me. A place where I can live with You forever. That during and after this life, You and I can have unbroken companionship with each other.

People have let me down before, left me by the wayside. But I know that is not Your way. That is not how You deal with Your loved ones. So in these days, Lord, help me not to worry but to hang on to the hope that wherever You are, I also can be, not just now but forevermore. Amen.

KEEPING CALM

*He who is slow to anger has great understanding, but he
who is hasty of spirit exposes and exalts his folly. A calm
and undisturbed mind and heart are the life and health of
the body, but envy, jealousy, and wrath are like rottenness
of the bones. . . . Wisdom rests [silently] in the mind and
heart of him who has understanding, but that which is in
the inward part of [self-confident] fools is made known.*

PROVERBS 14:29–30, 33 AMPC

Lord, I'm looking for a calm life. But to get there, I need
Your help. So I ask You, Lord, to help me curb my anger.
To give me the patience to listen to what others have to
say before I begin to respond. To help me be confident
in the knowledge that You will help me understand the
situation and carefully weigh the wisdom You have planted
within me. That You will give me the courage to say the
right words or to remain silent.

No matter what is happening in my life, Lord, may
the only thing I display to others be the inner light You
have sparked and continue to nurture within me. Amen.

THE AUTHOR OF PEACE

*Finally, brethren, farewell (rejoice)! Be strengthened
(perfected, completed, made what you ought to be);
be encouraged and consoled and comforted; be of the
same [agreeable] mind one with another; live in peace,
and [then] the God of love [Who is the Source of
affection, goodwill, love, and benevolence toward men]
and the Author and Promoter of peace will be with you.*

2 CORINTHIANS 13:11 AMPC

Too many times, Lord, when I look at a situation, I think
of all the bad things that could happen. Before I know it,
I'm in panic mode, wondering when the things I imag-
ined *could* happen *will* happen. It's enough to drive a girl
crazy. But that's not what You would have me do. So I'm
coming to You, Lord, to ask You for the strength of Your
Son. Help me become the person You created me to be.
Give me the encouragement I need to live with others in
peace, to see the bright side of life, and to focus on You,
the God of love. For when I'm dwelling in peace, You, the
God of love and the Author of peace, will be with me. In
Jesus' name, amen.

A Peaceful Place

The hill and the watchtower will become barren
places forever, the joy of wild donkeys, and a pasture
for flocks, until the Spirit from heaven is poured
out on us. . . . Then justice will inhabit the wilderness,
and righteousness will dwell in the orchard. The result
of righteousness will be peace; the effect of righteousness
will be quiet confidence forever. Then my people will
dwell in a peaceful place, in safe and secure dwellings.

Isaiah 32:14–18 hcsb

Your Spirit has poured down upon Your people, Lord God. That is the wonder of what Your Son, Jesus, has done for we who believe. That, Lord, is why I can find peace and order in this world of chaos. That is why I can now find so many good things to focus on in this life. That is why I can put aside any worries I may have. For trusting and obeying You and walking Your way has given me a quiet confidence. Following You has allowed me to live in this peaceful place where I know I am forever safe and secure in You. Amen.

STAND STRAIGHT

One Sabbath day as Jesus was teaching in a synagogue, he saw a woman who had been crippled by an evil spirit. She had been bent double for eighteen years and was unable to stand up straight. When Jesus saw her, he called her over and said, "Dear woman, you are healed of your sickness!" Then he touched her, and instantly she could stand straight. How she praised God!

LUKE 13:10–13 NLT

My fretting has become a real problem, Lord. My worries for the people of this world, especially the ones I love, have become such a heavy weight on my heart, mind, soul, and spirit. Yet You don't mean for me to carry this weight. You didn't design Your people to carry the burdens of the world upon their shoulders. So help me, Lord, to give all my worries over to You. Help me to allow every concern I have to simply slide off my back so that I can stand straight, lift up my eyes to You, and see all You have for Your people of peace. Touch me, heal me of this bad habit, Lord. I thank and praise You! Amen.

Straight Paths

*Lean on, trust in, and be confident in the Lord
with all your heart and mind and do not rely on your
own insight or understanding. In all your ways know,
recognize, and acknowledge Him, and He will direct
and make straight and plain your paths. Be not wise
in your own eyes; reverently fear and worship the
Lord and turn [entirely] away from evil.*

Proverbs 3:5–7 ampc

Lord, I've been putting my confidence in the wrong things—my own ideas, insights, and understanding. It's as if I'm trusting my own thoughts over Yours! Yet mine are so flawed and Yours are so perfect. Heaven help me, Lord!

Author of my life, help me to lean on and trust in You and Your Word with all my heart and mind. Help me to remember that *You* hold all wisdom and I don't. Help me, Lord, to acknowledge You every step of my way. Help me to recognize where You are working and to meet You there. Help me to follow Your promptings instead of my own whims. For then I know I will be walking Your way, following Your path. Amen.

Unshakable and Assured

Jesus answered them, "Do you finally believe? In fact,
you're about to make a run for it—saving your own
skins and abandoning me. But I'm not abandoned.
The Father is with me. I've told you all this so that trusting
me, you will be unshakable and assured, deeply at peace.
In this godless world you will continue to experience
difficulties. But take heart! I've conquered the world."
John 16:31–33 msg

I'm looking for that perfect peace, Jesus, the peace You alone can provide me, the peace You alone modeled when You walked this earth. Somehow, with everything You faced, everything You went through, You maintained that peace, that calm, that presence of mind. So help me now, Lord, to obtain and sustain that same peace. Remind me that You will never abandon me. I will never be all alone. Trusting You, I will be unshakable, unmovable, and deeply at peace. And even though I may continue to have difficulties and hardships, no matter what comes my way I can and will take heart because You have conquered all. Amen.

Precious Peace

Humble yourselves under the mighty power of God,
and at the right time he will lift you up in honor. Give all
your worries and cares to God, for he cares about you.
Stay alert! Watch out for your great enemy, the devil.
He prowls around like a roaring lion, looking for someone
to devour. Stand firm against him, and be strong in your
faith. . . . Peace be with all of you who are in Christ.
1 Peter 5:6–9, 14 nlt

Lord, it seems as if the world keeps getting more complicated and difficult. Some days the weight of it drags me down. But then I turn to Your words and my mind is set right.

Thank You, God, for Your loving presence in my life, for accepting me, helping me, taking care of me. Thank You for taking all my worries and woes into Your own hands. My desire is to stick to You like glue. So help me to stay alert, Lord, and to stand firm against the evil in this world. Help me to stay strong in my faith so that I can experience Your precious peace as I live and breathe in Christ. Amen.

ON YOUR SIDE

*The Lord is on my side; I will not fear. What can man
do to me? The Lord is on my side and takes my part,
He is among those who help me; therefore shall I see
my desire established upon those who hate me. It is
better to trust and take refuge in the Lord than to put
confidence in man. It is better to trust and take refuge
in the Lord than to put confidence in princes.*

PSALM 118:6–9 AMPC

Lord, with You on my side, I can do anything You call me
to do, no matter how difficult. With You, I fear no one
and nothing. When I need a safe and sure refuge, I know
You will be there for me, a secure place for me to run to.

So help me, Lord, to trust You more than anyone or
anything else. Help me not to depend on other people.
They are fallible, but You are not. You are the perfect and
incomparable God of all. It's You I look to as my safe
haven, You I trust with all I am and have, You I have
complete confidence in. In Jesus' name, amen.

BIRDS OF PRAISE

"Don't worry about your life, what you will eat or what you will drink; or about your body, what you will wear. Isn't life more than food and the body more than clothing? Look at the birds of the sky: They don't sow or reap or gather into barns, yet your heavenly Father feeds them. Aren't you worth more than they?"
MATTHEW 6:25–26 HCSB

Some days, Lord, I feel as if I'm living hand to mouth. That makes it hard to stay calm. Yet then I read in Your Word that I'm not to worry about my life, what I'll eat, drink, or wear. Because there is more to life than food, drink, and dress. And we are to trust You for everything!

Your birds are a great reminder that You will provide for Your creatures. For they neither plant nor harvest, yet You give them all they need! And in turn they physically praise You. For every time a bird lowers its beak to drink water, it then lifts its head to heaven—not only to take in the water but to look up to You! May we, Your children, do the same! Amen.

Like a Shepherd

Messenger of good news, shout from the
mountaintops! . . . Shout, and do not be afraid.
Tell the towns of Judah, "Your God is coming!" Yes,
the Sovereign Lord is coming in power. He will rule with
a powerful arm. See, he brings his reward with him as he
comes. He will feed his flock like a shepherd. He will carry
the lambs in his arms, holding them close to his heart.
He will gently lead the mother sheep with their young.

Isaiah 40:9–11 nlt

Lord, when I feel weak, I remember Your strength. When I feel alone, I know You are on Your way. You will remember, rescue, and revive me. No matter who or what comes against me, I know that You hold all the power, You are the Champion, You are the Victor in every way.

So please come, Lord—come to me now in all Your power. Bless me with Your presence, Good Shepherd. Nourish me, carry me in Your arms, hold me close to Your heart. Get a tight grip on me and never let me go. For I need Your gentle touch, Your guidance, care, and protection. In Jesus' name, amen.

Seeing Jesus

*Our great power is from God, not from ourselves. We are
pressed on every side by troubles, but we are not crushed.
We are perplexed, but not driven to despair. We are hunted
down, but never abandoned by God. We get knocked down,
but we are not destroyed. Through suffering, our bodies
continue to share in the death of Jesus so that the life
of Jesus may also be seen in our bodies.*

2 Corinthians 4:7–10 nlt

No matter how hard things get, Lord, I know that everything will be okay. That's because Your power resides within me. That's why, even though troubles surround me, they won't crush me. Even though I may get confused at times, I won't freak out entirely. And even though others may make things difficult for me because of my faith, I know You will always be with me. When I get knocked down, I am able to rise again. I'm not worried about what others can do to me, because I know what You've already done for me. And that makes every day worth living. For from sunrise to sunset, I have the chance to help others see You through me. In Jesus' name, amen.

An Encamped Angel

I sought (inquired of) the Lord and required Him
[of necessity and on the authority of His Word],
and He heard me, and delivered me from all my fears. . . .
The Angel of the Lord encamps around those who fear
Him [who revere and worship Him with awe] and each
of them He delivers. O taste and see that the Lord [our
God] is good! Blessed (happy, fortunate, to be envied)
is the man who trusts and takes refuge in Him.

Psalm 34:4, 7–8 ampc

When fears assail me, Lord, I look for You. I seek Your face, knowing my need is great and only You can fill it. So here I am, Lord. Hear my prayer. Save me from drowning in fears, none of which serve me. Remind me of who You are and what You do. For Your angel puts a circle of protection around me, keeping me safe from all harm. So I'm entrusting myself and my loved ones to You, Lord. For You are so much bigger than any fears riddling me. Blessed am I, a woman who trusts You and runs to You for refuge. In Jesus' name, amen.

GOD'S GOT YOU

*Let your character or moral disposition be free from love
of money [including greed, avarice, lust, and craving for
earthly possessions] and be satisfied with your present
[circumstances and with what you have]; for He [God]
Himself has said, I will not in any way fail you nor give you
up nor leave you without support. [I will] not, [I will] not,
[I will] not in any degree leave you helpless nor forsake nor
let [you] down (relax My hold on you)! [Assuredly not!]*
HEBREWS 13:5 AMPC

It's hard not to worry, Lord, when I have money issues.
It's not that I love money. I just worry that I won't have
enough to pay the bills when they come due. Help me,
Lord, to trust You more and more every day. Help me to
be satisfied with what I have, with my present blessings,
because You, Lord, have promised—You have said again
and again—that You will never fail me. You will always
be there to sustain me. You will never leave me without
resources. You will never let me fall or relax Your hold on
me. Thank You! Amen.

LOOK UP

I look up to the mountains—does my help come from
there? My help comes from the LORD, who made heaven
and earth! He will not let you stumble; the one who watches
over you will not slumber. . . . The LORD stands beside you
as your protective shade. The sun will not harm you by day,
nor the moon at night. The LORD keeps you from all harm
and watches over your life. The LORD keeps watch over
you as you come and go, both now and forever.
PSALM 121:1–3, 5–8 NLT

I look all around me, Lord, yet I see no hope. Discouraged, I bow my head and pray. And as I pray, I remember who You are, where You are. Amid a bevy of unspoken words, I look up to the mountains, to the sky. And there lie my hope and my help. They come from You, the One who made heaven and earth and me! You won't let me trip up, for You're watching over me. You have a plan and a purpose for all things, including me. And in that assurance, I rest in You, knowing You will keep me safe both now and forever. Amen.

HEART'S DESIRES

*Don't worry about the wicked or envy those who do wrong.
For like grass, they soon fade away. Like spring flowers,
they soon wither. Trust in the LORD and do good. Then you
will live safely in the land and prosper. Take delight in the
LORD, and he will give you your heart's desires.*

PSALM 37:1–4 NLT

Sometimes, Lord, it seems as if those who are not Your
children get all the breaks, money, and success they want.
And those of us who are following You, working to do
good and to love others, get the short end of the stick.
But then I come to Your Word and I'm reminded that
those who do wrong will not live forever in You. They
will go the way of all those who have no interest in You.
No matter what rewards they may get on earth, I know
mine are awaiting me in heaven. So while I'm here, I'll
trust in You and do what You created me to do. I'll delight
in Your trustworthy presence, depending on You for all
I need. Then, even here, You will give me what my heart
desires. In Jesus' name, amen.

Transformed

*I plead with you to give your bodies to God because of
all he has done for you. Let them be a living and holy
sacrifice—the kind he will find acceptable. This is truly the
way to worship him. Don't copy the behavior and customs
of this world, but let God transform you into a new person
by changing the way you think. Then you will learn to know
God's will for you, which is good and pleasing and perfect.*

ROMANS 12:1–2 NLT

Lord, sometimes when things seem off-kilter in my life,
I have to stop in my tracks and look in the mirror. That's
when I realize I'm slipping, looking to be a woman who
copies the styles and fads of this world instead of the
woman *You* want me to be, the woman You *created* me to
be. A woman of Christ.

So here I am before You, Lord. Help me to stop
looking to the world as my guide. Transform me into a
new woman, *Your* woman, by changing the way I think.
For then I will find that beautiful woman You created me
to be, the one who worships You and is transformed in
You. In Jesus' name, amen.

In Returning

Thus said the Lord God, the Holy One of Israel:
In returning [to Me] and resting [in Me] you shall be
saved; in quietness and in [trusting] confidence shall
be your strength. . . . Blessed (happy, fortunate, to be
envied) are all those who [earnestly] wait for Him,
who expect and look and long for Him [for His victory,
His favor, His love, His peace, His joy, and His
matchless, unbroken companionship]!

ISAIAH 30:15, 18 AMPC

I need You, Lord. When the day's worries about the present and the night's fears about the future begin to consume me, I come to You. For only by returning to You and resting in You will I be saved from all the fretting and fuming that nags and gnaws at my spirit. I will be strengthened when I lie down, quietly and confidently trusting in You. Happy I am as I wait for You, looking for and longing for Your presence, Your blessing, Your love, Your joy, Your peace, and best of all, Your companionship. What more could a woman ask? In Jesus' name, amen.

THE SOLID ROCK

Is there any god like GOD? Are we not at bedrock?
Is not this the God who armed me well, then aimed me
in the right direction? Now I run like a deer; I'm king
of the mountain. He shows me how to fight; I can bend
a bronze bow! You protect me with salvation-armor;
you touch me and I feel ten feet tall. You cleared the
ground under me so my footing was firm.

2 SAMUEL 22:32–37 MSG

Today I praise You, Lord, for all You are to me. You are a solid rock, a stable and immovable pillar for me in an unsteady world. You are the One I can run to for protection and strength. With You within me, I can do anything You've called me to do. You are the One who sets me free, who guides me in the right direction, who puts me on the best path. You make my feet like those of a deer so that I can climb mountains without missing a step. You defend me and raise me up to heights I've never known before. What a wonderful Lord You are! Amen.

BLESSED BECAUSE YOU BELIEVE

At the sound of Mary's greeting, Elizabeth's child leaped within her, and Elizabeth was filled with the Holy Spirit. Elizabeth gave a glad cry and exclaimed to Mary, "God has blessed you above all women, and your child is blessed. Why am I so honored, that the mother of my Lord should visit me? When I heard your greeting, the baby in my womb jumped for joy. You are blessed because you believed that the Lord would do what he said."

LUKE 1:41–45 NLT

When worries crowd my mind, Lord, I feel anything but blessed. Thoughts of my troubles tend to leak into my soul and weigh down my spirit. But then I am reminded of Your promise never to leave me. To do the impossible in and through me. To be with me always. To fill me with Your presence. So I ask You, Lord, to tell me today what promise You would have me hold on to in this moment, knowing I will be blessed—blessed because I believe You will actually do all You say You'll do. In Jesus' name, amen.

LEANING ON GOD

*Commit your way to the Lord [roll and repose
each care of your load on Him]; trust (lean on, rely on,
and be confident) also in Him and He will bring it to
pass. . . . Be still and rest in the Lord; wait for Him
and patiently lean yourself upon Him; fret not yourself
because of him who prospers in his way, because of
the man who brings wicked devices to pass.*

PSALM 37:5, 7 AMPC

All the concerns I hold deep in my heart, Lord, I turn over
to You. For although I cannot carry this load, I know You
can. So I'm trusting You and placing in Your care all my
loved ones, all I need, and all I have. I'm committing to
You all my hopes, dreams, and wishes. For I am confident
You will help me as I walk this road with You.

And now, Lord, in this moment of stillness, I relax
in You, leaning back upon You, resting my head on Your
shoulder. I'm quieting myself before You, allowing all
that troubles me to fade away, knowing You will deal with
those who rally against Your goodness. Amen.

COMPASSION

He [King Herod] sent and had John beheaded in the prison. . . . Now when Jesus heard this, he withdrew from there in a boat to a desolate place by himself. But when the crowds heard it, they followed him on foot from the towns. When he went ashore he saw a great crowd, and he had compassion on them and healed their sick.

MATTHEW 14:10, 13–14 ESV

I want to be like You, Lord. When You heard about Your cousin John the Baptist, You stepped away for a bit by Yourself. Yet when others came to be blessed or healed by You and followed You, You had compassion on them and healed them.

Help me, Lord, to be as selfless as You. Make me a woman who has the capacity to put her own troubles aside and help those in need. Give me that kind of heart, that kind of energy, that kind of empathy, that kind of desire. Fill me with Your spirit of kindness and compassion so that I may serve You as You served others. Amen.

A Voice behind You

O people who dwell in Zion at Jerusalem, you will weep no more. He will surely be gracious to you at the sound of your cry; when He hears it, He will answer you. . . . Your Teacher will not hide Himself any more, but your eyes will constantly behold your Teacher. And your ears will hear a word behind you, saying, This is the way; walk in it, when you turn to the right hand and when you turn to the left.

ISAIAH 30:19–21 AMPC

Lord, I'm tired of crying, "Woe is me." I don't know how or why I ever adopted that mindset, because I know that is not what You want for me. So I'm calling out to You for help, knowing You will answer me. My eyes and mind are going to focus on You. My ears are open to Your voice, instruction, and guidance. At all my crossroads, when I have a choice to go right or left, Lord, tell me which way to go, which way You would have me walk. I will listen for You to say, "This is the way; walk in it"—and I will go willingly.

WHOLLY LEANING

*We take comfort and are encouraged and confidently
and boldly say, The Lord is my Helper; I will not be seized
with alarm.... What can man do to me? Remember your
leaders and superiors in authority.... Imitate their faith
(their conviction that God exists and is the Creator and
Ruler of all things, the Provider and Bestower of eternal
salvation through Christ, and their leaning of the entire
human personality on God in absolute trust and
confidence in His power, wisdom, and goodness).*

HEBREWS 13:6–7 AMPC

Lord, I realize I do lean on You for some things, handing
You my concerns in certain areas. But I have yet to lean
my entire self upon You. For some reason, I find myself
holding part of me back. So help me, Lord, to trust fully
in You. Remind me that because You are my Helper, I
need not be worried about or afraid of anything.

You, Lord, are the Creator of this universe. You sustain it all. You, the mightiest of all, rule over every people
and every big and little thing. So in this moment, in this
time and place, I give You all of me, Lord. Today I place
myself and my total trust and confidence in You, Your
power, Your wisdom, and Your goodness. Amen.

GOD PLANS FOR GOOD

*Joseph said to them, "Don't be afraid. Am I in the place
of God? You planned evil against me; God planned it for
good to bring about the present result—the survival of
many people. Therefore don't be afraid. I will take care
of you and your little ones." And he comforted them.*
GENESIS 50:19–21 HCSB

There are times in my life, Lord, when I find myself snared
in the evil plans of others. And part of me wants to seek
vengeance. But then I remember what happened to Joseph
so many thousands of years ago. How he never asked
why he was in certain predicaments but just did the best
he could whenever and wherever he could because he
knew *You were* with him. And in the end, although his
brothers had planned evil against him, God made all
come out good, not just for Joseph but for many other
people.

So I'm determined, Lord, not to seek revenge. Instead I will simply look for You in the midst of all that's
happening, knowing You will bring good out of whatever
evil is happening. In Jesus' name I live and pray, amen.

SAFE PLACE

Keep and protect me, O God, for in You I have found
refuge, and in You do I put my trust and hide myself.
I say to the Lord, You are my Lord; I have no good
beside or beyond You. . . . The Lord is my chosen and
assigned portion, my cup; You hold and maintain
my lot. The lines have fallen for me in pleasant
places; yes, I have a good heritage.

PSALM 16:1–2, 5–6 AMPC

Lord, without You in my life, all is chaos. I have no comfort. Worries drag me down. I do nothing but sigh in consternation. That's why I run to You each and every day. Keep and protect me, Lord. Be my safe place of refuge. Let me catch my breath as I lean into You, trusting You with everything I am and have.

You, Lord, are the best thing in my life. When I feel as if I'm being pulled in ten different directions, I come to You. And You calm me down, give me the peace, comfort, and wisdom I need. Thank You for being with me and taking care of me. Because of You, I have a lovely life. In Jesus' name, amen.

No Other God

*Shadrach, Meshach, and Abednego replied,
"O Nebuchadnezzar, we do not need to defend
ourselves before you. If we are thrown into the blazing
furnace, the God whom we serve is able to save us.
He will rescue us from your power, Your Majesty.
But even if he doesn't, we want to make it clear to you,
Your Majesty, that we will never serve your gods
or worship the gold statue you have set up."*
Daniel 3:16–18 nlt

Whenever the going gets tough, Lord, I need an extra dose of help. From You I need the faith to defy those who force me to do what is against Your will and way. Help me to stand up for myself and stick close to You, knowing that the threats of others are nothing to me because I have You in my life. Remind me that You will be with me whether I am rescued in this world or not. No matter what happens, I will follow and obey You alone. For You are my true and only God, the all-powerful, all-knowing Savior whom I will love and serve in this life and the next.

AMID THE FLAMES

So Shadrach, Meshach, and Abednego, securely tied,
fell into the roaring flames. But suddenly, Nebuchadnezzar
...exclaimed to his advisers, "Didn't we tie up three men
and throw them into the furnace?" "Yes, Your Majesty,
we certainly did," they replied. "Look!" Nebuchadnezzar
shouted. "I see four men, unbound, walking around in the
fire unharmed! And the fourth looks like a god!" ...
Then Nebuchadnezzar said, "Praise to the God of
Shadrach, Meshach, and Abednego! He sent his angel
to rescue his servants who trusted in him."

DANIEL 3:23–25, 28 NLT

When I'm feeling troubled or find myself in the midst
of a crisis, give me the courage, Lord, to stay strong in
You. Help me to stay on Your path, follow Your will,
seek only Your way. For I know that no matter what happens, whether I be walking amid the flames or swim-
ming against the tides, You will be walking and striving
with me, giving me the comfort and wisdom I need to
not just survive but thrive. For it is when I don't let my
troubles, worries, and crises get me down that the true
miracle of Your power and presence is seen. Amen.

THE TRUE PATH

*I will praise the LORD who counsels me—even at
night my conscience instructs me. I keep the LORD in
mind always. Because He is at my right hand, I will
not be shaken. Therefore my heart is glad and my spirit
rejoices; my body also rests securely. . . . You reveal the
path of life to me; in Your presence is abundant joy;
in Your right hand are eternal pleasures.*

PSALM 16:7–9, 11 HCSB

My true path is discovered, Lord, when I look to You for
all things. When I seek Your wisdom. When I hear Your
voice speaking to my heart at night. That's why I want to
keep You, Your Word, and Your Spirit always with me.
With You in my midst, nothing can shake me up, bring
me down, or turn me around.

I am amazed at the peace that You and Your presence
give me, Lord. You make my heart glad. Joy springs from
my lips. I burst into songs of praise. For You make me
feel as light as a leaf upon the wind. Because of You, I
find the rest and safety and clear path I need to live this
life for You. Amen.

No Hesitation

When Lot still hesitated, the angels seized his hand
and the hands of his wife and two daughters and
rushed them to safety outside the city, for the LORD
was merciful. . . . One of the angels ordered, "Run for
your lives! And don't look back or stop anywhere in the
valley! Escape to the mountains, or you will be swept
away!" . . . But Lot's wife looked back as she was
following behind him, and she turned into a pillar of salt.

GENESIS 19:16–17, 26 NLT

Lord, when I'm heading for trouble because my feet are planted too firmly in the ground, help me to move out with no hesitation. To trust You and whatever messengers You send to rescue me. Help me, Lord, to understand that no matter what is happening in my life, You are watching over me with love, mercy, and compassion. Help me to lift my lead feet, to move forward, to run for my life, and to never look back, longing for what I once had. Help me always to "remember what happened to Lot's wife!" (Luke 17:32 NLT). Amen.

LOVING COMMANDS

Just then an expert in the law stood up to test Him, saying,
"Teacher, what must I do to inherit eternal life?" "What is
written in the law?" He asked him. "How do you read it?"
He answered: Love the Lord your God with all your heart,
with all your soul, with all your strength, and with all your
mind; and your neighbor as yourself. "You've answered
correctly," He told him. "Do this and you will live."

LUKE 10:25–28 HCSB

I know Your two commandments, Lord Jesus, the ones
that tell me I'm to love the Father with all my heart, soul,
and mind and I'm to love my neighbor as myself.

Not once did You say worries will help me inherit
eternal life. So help me break the fretting frenzy. Help
me to let my worries about the past, present, and future
fade away. Wasting my time being consumed by fears,
concerns, and anxieties just depletes the energy I need to
follow Your loving commands. But to get to that worry-
free place, Lord, I need and now request the gift of Your
calm, Your peace, and Your presence, in this moment
and every moment to come. Amen.

A Prayer Habit

*The administrators and high officers went to the king
and said, . . . "Give orders that. . .any person who prays to
anyone, divine or human—except to you, Your Majesty—
will be thrown into the den of lions." . . . So King Darius
signed the law. But when Daniel learned that the law had
been signed, he went home and knelt down as usual in his
upstairs room. . . . He prayed three times a day, just as he
had always done, giving thanks to his God.*

DANIEL 6:6–7, 9–10 NLT

I want to have a powerful prayer life like Daniel, Lord.
No matter what, he stayed committed to You and so was
supported and protected by You. Because Daniel bowed
down to You, kneeling in prayer before You, this faithful
follower was able to rise above his trials and those trying
to bring him down.

So help me, Lord, to get into my own prayer habit.
Prompt me to meet You at the same time and place every
day. To be committed to doing so. Then I too, as I bow
down to You, will be able to rise above whatever comes
my way. Amen.

The Good Portion

*Mary. . .seated herself at the Lord's feet and was listening
to His teaching. But Martha [overly occupied and too
busy] was distracted with much serving; and she. . .said,
Lord, is it nothing to You that my sister has left me to serve
alone? . . . The Lord replied. . .Martha, Martha, you are
anxious and troubled about many things; there is need of
only one or but a few things. Mary has chosen the good
portion. . .which shall not be taken away from her.*
Luke 10:39–42 ampc

Too often, Lord, I feel like I'm a Martha. I have good
intentions at the beginning of the day. I am quiet and
focused on You, attending to Your will and way. But then
the next thing I know, I'm caught up in a flurry of activity,
and whatever sense I had of Your presence has flown out
of the window! I don't want to live that kind of life, Lord,
where my anxieties, concerns, and troubles crowd in on
me and crowd You out. Help me, Lord, to choose that
good portion, the one where I sit at Your feet, undistracted
and captured by Your words and presence. Amen.

WARRIOR VERSUS WORRIER

A stone was brought and placed over the mouth of the den. . . . Very early the next morning, the king got up. . . . "Daniel, servant of the living God! Was your God, whom you serve so faithfully, able to rescue you from the lions?" Daniel answered, . . ."My God sent his angel to shut the lions' mouths so that they would not hurt me." . . . Not a scratch was found on him, for he had trusted in his God.

DANIEL 6:17, 19–23 NLT

Lord, no matter what happens in my life, help me to trust in You completely. Help me to walk with You so closely, to serve You so faithfully that not one bump in the road, not one word of discouragement, not one setback, not one sign of trouble will keep me from following wherever You lead, from doing whatever You would have me do, from serving whenever You want me to serve. Give me the strength of heart to be a woman warrior, not a fretful female. For my heart's desire is to live a life of confidence, not cowardice. In Jesus' name I pray, amen.

SITTING BY THE ROADSIDE

Bartimaeus, a blind beggar, a son of Timaeus, was sitting
by the roadside. And when he heard that it was Jesus of
Nazareth, he began to shout, saying, Jesus, Son of David,
have pity and mercy pity on me [now]! And many severely
censured and reproved him, telling him to keep still,
but he kept on shouting out all the more, You Son
of David, have pity and mercy on me [now]!

MARK 10:46–48 AMPC

Sometimes I find myself sitting on the sidelines, wondering how I will ever get rid of all that plagues me. I wonder when I will see the solution to my problems or have enough to see me through more than a day. And then I realize You, Lord Jesus, are so very near. Although I cannot see You, I feel Your presence. That's when I begin to shout out for You! I ask for Your love, compassion, and mercy. I ignore the tumult around me, focusing on You alone. Lord, I beg You, help me! Free me from my cares and concerns as I seek to draw ever closer to You. Amen.

Spiritual Eyesight

Jesus stopped and said, Call him. And they called the
blind man, telling him, Take courage! Get up! He is calling
you. And throwing off his outer garment, he leaped up and
came to Jesus. And Jesus said to him, What do you want
Me to do for you? And the blind man said to Him, Master,
let me receive my sight. And Jesus said to him, Go your
way; your faith has healed you. And at once he received
his sight and accompanied Jesus on the road.

Mark 10:49–52 ampc

Thank You, Lord, for stopping for me, for calling me. Seeking Your presence, I take up my courage and I throw off everything—troubles, pride, worries, sins—that might hinder my running to You. When I reach Your side, You ask me, "What do you want Me to do for you?" And my answer is clear and true. "Lord, let me see You. Open my spiritual eyes to You, Your ways, and Your truth."

Then I hear You say, "Go your way; your faith has healed you." And at once I can see You. Not wanting to leave Your side, I follow You down the road, never to part from You. Amen.

THE RIGHT PATH

Show me the right path, O LORD; point out the
road for me to follow. Lead me by your truth and
teach me, for you are the God who saves me.
All day long I put my hope in you. Remember, O LORD,
your compassion and unfailing love, which you have
shown from long ages past. Do not remember the
rebellious sins of my youth. Remember me in the light
of your unfailing love, for you are merciful, O LORD.

PSALM 25:4–7 NLT

When I don't know the right way to go, I turn to You, O Lord. For Your knowledge and wisdom are deep. You can see the way that lies before me. You know where I've come from, the trials and troubles I've endured.

So, dear Lord, lead me by Your truth. Teach me all I need to know so that I can rest, stop, or turn to the right or left, wherever You bid me go—or not go. I'm looking for a fresh outpouring of the love You've always held for me, Lord. Rain it down upon me now so that I will find the strength and energy and wisdom to do as You will.

BOLD AND BELIEVING FAITH

*Two blind men followed along behind him, shouting,
"Son of David, have mercy on us!" They went right
into the house where he was staying, and Jesus asked
them, "Do you believe I can make you see?" "Yes, Lord,"
they told him, "we do." Then he touched their eyes
and said, "Because of your faith, it will happen."
Then their eyes were opened, and they could see!*

MATTHEW 9:27–30 NLT

You know who I am, Lord. You know the struggles I've had, the challenges I have overcome. My concern is that I seem to believe more in my own powers than Yours. In other words, I need a faith lift.

Help me, Lord, to rely on You, have faith in You, and trust in You. Give me the boldness to follow You, shouting out that I need Your mercy, Your compassion, Your support. Help me to see that You are the answer to all my questions, the source of all I need. And when You ask me if I believe You can help me, may I say, "Yes, Lord, yes!" For I know that because of my faith, what I desire will be provided. Amen.

A Friend in Deed

*Who are those who fear the LORD? He will show them
the path they should choose. They will live in prosperity,
and their children will inherit the land. The LORD is a
friend to those who fear him. He teaches them his covenant.
My eyes are always on the LORD, for he rescues me from
the traps of my enemies. Turn to me and have mercy,
for I am alone and in deep distress. My problems go
from bad to worse. Oh, save me from them all!*

PSALM 25:12–17 NLT

Here I stand before You, Lord, waiting for a good word
to fall from Your lips and into my ear. I'm waiting for
You, Lord, to give me the direction I need, to tell me
the words that will soothe my soul and give me hope.
For You, Lord God, are my Comforter, Friend, Beloved,
Helper, Counselor, and Refuge. My eyes are constantly
on You, for You hold all wisdom and power. You are the
One who rescues me from evil. So look upon me now,
Lord; see how deeply distressed I am in heart and spirit.
Save me from all my problems and lift me to Your place
of peace.

LIKE SHEEP

I am sending you out like sheep in the midst of wolves. . . .
Be on guard against men [whose way or nature is to
act in opposition to God]. . . . When they deliver you up,
do not be anxious about how or what you are to speak;
for what you are to say will be given you in that very
hour and moment, for it is not you who are speaking,
but the Spirit of your Father speaking through you.
MATTHEW 10:16–17, 19–20 AMPC

Father God, I have found that being a Christian is definitely not a walk in the park—but it's still so much better than any other path. Besides, it is the only path that is right and true! Yet here You are, sending me out like a sheep in the midst of wolves. Still, I won't worry, for when fear begins to creep in, You, the Good Shepherd, have promised to be right here with me. No matter what happens, I don't need to be anxious or worried, terrified or distressed. I don't even need to worry about what to say when I'm questioned, for Your Spirit will speak through me. What more could a little ewe ask?

ABUNDANT PEACE

Refrain from anger, and forsake wrath! Fret not yourself;
it tends only to evil. For the evildoers shall be cut off,
but those who wait for the LORD shall inherit the land.
In just a little while, the wicked will be no more; though
you look carefully at his place, he will not be there.
But the meek shall inherit the land and delight
themselves in abundant peace.

PSALM 37:8–11 ESV

Sometimes, Lord, I get so upset about the ne'er-do-wells who, while evading laws and plotting who knows what, end up looking like winners in this society. Meanwhile, Your followers are being taken advantage of, living from hand to mouth, having to struggle for what others get handed to them. It just doesn't seem fair. At the same time, I realize You don't want me to get upset about wrongdoers. I know if my frustration and anger continue to grow, I myself might end up drifting away from You. So I'm going to wait on You, Lord. You promise that evildoers will one day be no more. But Your meek and loving followers not only will have deeds to the land but will live in Your abundant peace. In Jesus' name, amen.

THE SHEPHERD
WHO CARRIES YOU

The Lord is my Strength and my [impenetrable] Shield; my heart trusts in, relies on, and confidently leans on Him, and I am helped; therefore my heart greatly rejoices, and with my song will I praise Him. The Lord is their [unyielding] Strength, and He is the Stronghold of salvation to [me] His anointed. Save Your people and bless Your heritage; nourish and shepherd them and carry them forever.

PSALM 28:7–9 AMPC

When I am weak, Lord, You are my Strength. When I am too fragile to protect myself, You are my Shield. In You alone my heart trusts. On You alone I rely. Because I cannot do all things in my own power, I clamor for Your help. Because You are my all in all, I cannot help but sing songs of rejoicing, praising You. For You are the One who saves me from all snares, and even from myself! Yes, Lord, You are my perfect peace.

Thank You, my Strength and Shield, for blessing and preserving me; for continually nourishing me; for being the Shepherd who carries me, in this life and the next. Amen.

Relief and Refreshment

*Come to Me, all you who labor and are heavy-laden
and overburdened, and I will cause you to rest. [I will ease
and relieve and refresh your souls.] Take My yoke upon
you and learn of Me, for I am gentle (meek) and humble
(lowly) in heart, and you will find rest (relief and ease
and refreshment and recreation and blessed quiet) for your
souls. For My yoke is wholesome (useful, good—not harsh,
hard, sharp, or pressing, but comfortable, gracious, and
pleasant), and My burden is light and easy to be borne.*
MATTHEW 11:28–30 AMPC

Lord, when I am tired and weary of carrying my burdens
upon my own back, finally realizing how much I have
picked up along the way, I come to You. For You will give
me the rest I need. You will relieve and refresh my soul.

Teach me, Lord Jesus, what You would have me know.
Show me what You would have me see. Then I will find
the peace and quiet You promise to those who come to
You and comfort themselves in You. Then I will find the
"unforced rhythms of [Your] grace" (Matthew 11:29 MSG).
In Your name I pray, amen.

THE STEPS OF A GOOD WOMAN

*For such as are blessed of God shall [in the end] inherit
the earth.... The steps of a [good] man are directed and
established by the Lord when He delights in his way [and
He busies Himself with his every step]. Though he falls,
he shall not be utterly cast down, for the Lord grasps his
hand in support and upholds him.... Depart from evil
and do good; and you will dwell forever [securely].*

PSALM 37:22–24, 27 AMPC

Lord, I am so thankful that You have promised to walk
with me every step of the way. That You will actually direct
my path because I am Your child and am committed to do
good in Your name. Even if I trip up, if I make a mistake
or take a misstep, I won't be down forever. For You will
be right there beside me. You, like any good parent, will
grab my hand, lift me up, and set me back on my feet.
Thank You, Lord, for all You have done and promise to
continue to do in, through, and for me. Amen.

STOP DOING, JUST BE

The apostles [sent out as missionaries] came back and
gathered together to Jesus, and told Him all that they
had done and taught. And He said to them, [As for you]
come away by yourselves to a deserted place, and rest a
while—for many were [continually] coming and going,
and they had not even leisure enough to eat. And they
went away in a boat to a solitary place by themselves.

MARK 6:30–32 AMPC

I am strung so tightly, Lord. I have been running around
like a madwoman, trying to meet all my deadlines, perform all my duties, do all that is expected of me. But this
busyness, this idea of being a superwoman who feels she
has to do it all, is definitely taking a toll on me. So I come
to You, Lord Jesus, in response to Your invitation. I'm
ready to come away with You, alone, to a deserted place,
and rest. For I cannot and am not made to keep up this
kind of pace. I'm ready to get into a boat with You and
sail away to a remote spot where I can stop doing and just
be with You alone. Amen.

STRENGTH AND PEACE

Ascribe to the Lord, O sons of the mighty,
ascribe to the Lord glory and strength. Give to the
Lord the glory due to His name; worship the Lord in
the beauty of holiness or in holy array.... The voice of the
Lord is powerful; the voice of the Lord is full of majesty....
The Lord [still] sits as King [and] forever! The Lord
will give [unyielding and impenetrable] strength to His
people; the Lord will bless His people with peace.
PSALM 29:1–2, 4, 10–11 AMPC

You, Lord, have such strength. Even Your voice can do tremendous things—break cedars, flash lightning, make the woods tremble, strip forests bare. What power! What a thunderous noise You must make!

The blessing here is that You will give me, Your follower, Your lamb, strength to do what You have called me to do, to be what You have already designed me to be. The strength You give will be unyielding and impenetrable. And You will also bless me with the peace I crave. Sign me up, Lord! For with You walking beside me and filling me with such amazing strength, I can kiss my worries goodbye! Amen.

COME AHEAD!

Jesus was quick to comfort them. "Courage, it's me.
Don't be afraid." Peter, suddenly bold, said, "Master,
if it's really you, call me to come to you on the water."
He said, "Come ahead." Jumping out of the boat,
Peter walked on the water to Jesus. But when he looked
down at the waves churning beneath his feet, he lost his
nerve and started to sink. He cried, "Master, save me!"
Jesus didn't hesitate. He reached down and grabbed his hand.
MATTHEW 14:27–31 MSG

I don't know what gets into me, Lord, but sometimes I fail to have complete faith in You. I'm eager enough to get out of my comfort zone. But then once I take that first step of faith, I start looking around, wondering, *Who am I to be walking on water?* And that's when the trouble starts—for I've taken my eyes off You.

So help me, Lord, to ignore the wind and waves, or whatever is threatening to sink me. Help me to cling to You, no matter where I am or what I'm doing, knowing that after You have called me, You won't let me drown but will support my walk with You in every way You can.

ANOTHER CHANCE

I give you all the credit, GOD—you got me out of that
mess. . . . I yelled for help and you put me together. GOD,
you pulled me out of the grave, gave me another chance at
life when I was down-and-out. All you saints! Sing your
hearts out to GOD! Thank him to his face! He gets angry
once in a while, but across a lifetime there is only love.
The nights of crying your eyes out give way to days of laughter.

PSALM 30:1–5 MSG

In times past, Lord, when I was in big trouble, You rescued me. I cried out for help and You got me back on my feet. You gave me another chance when I was so far down there was no way to go but up. Thank You, Lord, for answering when I call. For giving me the peace I need to stay calm amid chaos. Although there are times when You may get angry, I know Your love for me will never cease to amaze me. And although sometimes I may shed tears in the nighttime hours, You always bring me joy in the morning. For that and so much more, I thank You! Amen.

OPEN EYES

Jesus acted as if he were going on, but they begged him,
"Stay the night with us, since it is getting late." So he went
home with them. As they sat down to eat, he took the
bread and blessed it. Then he broke it and gave it to them.
Suddenly, their eyes were opened, and they recognized him.
And at that moment he disappeared! They said to each
other, "Didn't our hearts burn within us as he talked with
us on the road and explained the Scriptures to us?"

LUKE 24:28–32 NLT

In times of worry and confusion, Lord, lead me into Your
Word. Reveal what You would have me know. Explain the
concepts and principles I have trouble understanding.
Open my eyes to all You want me to see.

Promise to stay with me, Lord Jesus, to never leave
me as I seek Your way in this world. For I need the unique
comfort I get from Your Word and presence. Help
me to understand Your ways, to recognize You and the
part You play in my life, in this world and in the next.
Make my heart burn within me when Your words of
wisdom become my epiphany. Amen.

From Mourning to Merriment

When things were going great I crowed, "I've got it made. I'm GOD's favorite. He made me king of the mountain." Then you looked the other way and I fell to pieces. I called out to you, GOD. . . . "Help me out of this!" You did it: you changed wild lament into whirling dance; you ripped off my black mourning band and decked me with wildflowers. I'm about to burst with song. . . . GOD, my God, I can't thank you enough.

PSALM 30:6–8, 10–12 MSG

Sometimes I get a little arrogant, Lord. I begin to brag about how I've got it made. The next thing I know, I've wandered away from You and disaster falls upon me. So, Lord God, I call out to You. I ask You to lift me above the worries, troubles, and cares of this world. To pull me back into Your sphere, Your Word, Your way.

Then, as suddenly as I call out, "Save me, Lord!" You change my loud wails into victory songs. You change my black dress of mourning into a gown of gladness. Soon I can't help but sing my song of thanksgiving to You, my Lord and Redeemer. Amen.

LEAP OF FAITH

*The Israelites were exceedingly frightened. . . . They said
to Moses, . . . It would have been better for us to serve the
Egyptians than to die in the wilderness. Moses told the
people, Fear not; stand still (firm, confident, undismayed)
and see the salvation of the Lord which He will work
for you today. For the Egyptians you have seen today
you shall never see again. The Lord will fight for you,
and you shall hold your peace and remain at rest.*

EXODUS 14:10–14 AMPC

There are times, Lord, when I step out in faith and suddenly
find myself between a rock and a hard place, filled with
fear. I begin thinking, *I was safer not stepping out! Why
did I ever take this leap of faith in the first place?* Yet that's
when You want me to have even *more* faith.

So tell me those words I long to hear, Lord. That all
I need to do is take courage, stand still, and watch You
work a miracle. That You will fight for me. That I'm simply to hold my peace and remain calm. For You are with
me. Amen.

Before and Behind

And the Angel of God Who went before the host
of Israel moved and went behind them; and the pillar
of the cloud went from before them and stood behind
them, coming between the host of Egypt and the host
of Israel. It was a cloud and darkness to the Egyptians,
but it gave light by night to the Israelites; and the one
host did not come near the other all night.

Exodus 14:19–20 ampc

There are so many things I love about You, Lord. And one of them is how You look after me. How You always go before me to check out what lies ahead. At the same time, You've got my back by serving as a shield behind me. *And* You walk beside me, live within me, and sit above me. You are everywhere all the time. And not just for me, but for all my loved ones. Thank You, Lord, for standing between me and the darkness. Thank You, Lord, for being all the light I will ever need. In Jesus' name, amen.

A CONSTANT RETREAT READY

*A vast multitude, hearing all the many things that He was
doing, came to Him. And He told His disciples to have a
little boat in [constant] readiness for Him because of the
crowd, lest they press hard upon Him and crush Him.
For He had healed so many that all who had distressing
bodily diseases kept falling upon Him and pressing
upon Him in order that they might touch Him.*

MARK 3:8–10 AMPC

Lord, You are such a wonderful example to me. I want to
be sure to follow in Your footsteps, to imitate how You
lived, breathed, and moved through this world.

I've read how people who needed healing would form
a crowd and press against You. How they kept coming
after You, hoping for even the slightest touch of Your
hand or Your hem.

Please show me, Lord, how to make sure that I, Your
servant, have a continually ready retreat. A place where I
can go for rest—physically, mentally, spiritually, emotionally. A place where no one can reach me. A place where I
can find the peace I need to replenish my energy. Amen.

An Angel before You

*"See, I am sending an angel before you to protect you
on your journey and lead you safely to the place I have
prepared for you. Pay close attention to him, and obey
his instructions. Do not rebel against him, for he is my
representative, and he will not forgive your rebellion.
But if you are careful to obey him, following all my
instructions, then I will. . .oppose those who oppose you."*

<small>Exodus 23:20–22 nlt</small>

There are so many different ways You amaze me, Lord. You
have thought of everything to help me get through this
life on earth and ultimately to heaven with You. You have
sent an angel to go before me and protect me as I journey. And that same angel will lead me safely to the place
You have prepared for me. All I need to do is listen and
obey. If I do, then You will oppose all those who oppose
me! So many blessings in one pronouncement! So many
ways You have made sure I will safely reach my end goal—
an eternal life of peace with You, the God of all creation
who loves me unendingly. My Lord, I thank You. Amen.

A GREAT CALM

He [Himself] was in the stern [of the boat], asleep on
the [leather] cushion; and they awoke Him and said to
Him, Master, do You not care that we are perishing?
And He arose and rebuked the wind and said to the sea,
Hush now! Be still (muzzled)! And the wind ceased
(sank to rest as if exhausted by its beating) and there
was [immediately] a great calm (a perfect peacefulness).
He said to them, Why are you so timid and fearful?
How is it that you have no faith (no firmly relying trust)?
MARK 4:38–40 AMPC

At times, Lord, when I'm in trouble, when the waves
seem overwhelming and the wind unceasing, I begin to
panic, to give in to anxiety or fear, or to doubt Your saving
presence is with me. When the storm seems crushing and
untamable and the enemy tells me You will not be able to
save me, Lord, remind me that You have power over all
things. That all I need to do is trust that You will rise up
at the right moment, calm the storm, and still the chaos
within and without. Then Your peace will reign once more.
In Your name I pray, amen.

Meeting with the Lord

*I will meet with you to speak there to you. There I will
meet with the Israelites, and the Tent of Meeting shall
be sanctified by My glory [the Shekinah, God's visible
presence]. . . . And they shall know [from personal
experience] that I am the Lord their God, Who brought
them forth out of the land of Egypt that I might dwell
among them; I am the Lord their God.*

Exodus 29:42–43, 46 ampc

On days when peace seems elusive, I reach out to You,
dear Lord. I want to meet with You, speak with You, feel
Your presence. I want to see You, know all about You, and
have a personal experience with You.

You are my Lord. You are the One I worship, the
One I trust to fill the holes in my life. I want You to be
my constant Companion—my Provider, peace, Friend,
food, shelter, and shield. Dwell in my midst, Lord. Teach
me what I need to know. Be here in this moment, reach-
ing out for me as I reach out to You, spirit to Spirit, heart
to heart, breath to breath. Amen.

ANYTHING IS POSSIBLE

*"Have mercy on us and help us, if you can." "What do
you mean, 'If I can'?" Jesus asked. "Anything is possible
if a person believes." The father instantly cried out,
"I do believe, but help me overcome my unbelief!" . . .
Jesus. . .rebuked the evil spirit. . . . The boy appeared
to be dead. . . . But Jesus took him by the hand
and helped him to his feet, and he stood up.*
MARK 9:22–27 NLT

Lord Jesus, You are the worker of miracles. When everyone
has given up all hope, You come on the scene, hear our
requests, and answer in a power-filled way.

So here I am before You, Lord, with a problem.
My trust in You, my belief, may be less than either of us
would like. But it is there. And You have promised that
even with faith the size of a mere mustard seed, my prayer
will be answered. I believe You *can* do the impossible,
Lord. Do so now! Hear my prayer. Help me overcome
any unbelief I may have. And I will leave all the results
to You. In Your name I pray. Amen.

GOD GIVES YOU REST

Moses said to the LORD, "See, you say to me, 'Bring up
this people,' but you have not let me know whom you will
send with me. Yet you have said, 'I know you by name,
and you have also found favor in my sight.' Now therefore. . .
please show me now your ways, that I may know you
in order to find favor in your sight. . . ." And he said,
"My presence will go with you, and I will give you rest."
EXODUS 33:12–14 ESV

Lord, when I feel all alone, wondering how I will ever do
what You have called me to do, remind me that You are
with me. That Your actual presence is within my reach. That
the steps I take You are taking right along with me. And
that along this road, this pathway that we walk together,
You will give me the rest I need.

You know my name, Lord. You know everything
about me—my past and my future, my heartaches and
joys, my loves and losses. You know me like no other.
Help me to know You just as well, Lord. All so that I may
know how best to please You. Amen.

MOUNTAINOUS FAITH

Jesus, replying, said to them, Have faith in God [constantly].
Truly I tell you, whoever says to this mountain, Be lifted up
and thrown into the sea! and does not doubt at all in his
heart but believes that what he says will take place, it will
be done for him. For this reason I am telling you, whatever
you ask for in prayer, believe (trust and be confident)
that it is granted to you, and you will [get it].
MARK 11:22–24 AMPC

Lord, today I put all things—all my worries, concerns, plans, ideas, dreams, hopes, and aspirations and my whole self—into Your hands. I am determined to have constant faith in You.

You know all the obstacles that lie before me, Lord. You know the mountains I cannot get over, under, or around. Yet because of You and Your power, I know these hurdles will not remain here, blocking my path. I have no doubt in my heart that You will remove them for me because I am asking You to. I believe in Your mountain-moving power. And I have peace in my life, Lord, knowing there is nothing that You, my mighty God, cannot do. In Jesus' name, amen.

Bitter Juices

Whenever you stand praying, if you have anything against anyone, forgive him and let it drop (leave it, let it go), in order that your Father Who is in heaven may also forgive you your [own] failings and shortcomings and let them drop. But if you do not forgive, neither will your Father in heaven forgive your failings and shortcomings.

MARK 11:25–26 AMPC

There are people I need to forgive, Lord Jesus, but I'm having a hard time doing so. The wounds are either very fresh or very deep. The ironic thing about it is that while I remain stewing in my bitter juices, those I've not yet forgiven are going along their merry way, most likely having completely forgotten about the words or episode that created the divide.

At the same time, I know Father God won't forgive me unless I forgive those who've harmed me. So help me do so now, Lord Jesus. Help me bring all these names, faces, words, and incidents before You, drop them at Your feet, and leave them there, allowing only forgiveness to remain within my heart and upon my lips. In Your name and power I pray, amen.

The Sleep of Peace

*"If you follow my decrees and are careful to obey my
commands, I will send you the seasonal rains. The land
will then yield its crops, and the trees of the field will
produce their fruit.... I will give you peace in the land,
and you will be able to sleep with no cause for fear."*
LEVITICUS 26:3–4, 6 NLT

Some nights I have trouble sleeping, Lord. I have so
many worries on my mind. Sometimes I even find it difficult to think, to laugh, to enjoy my life, the life with
which You've blessed me.

Help me, Lord, to just look to You and follow Your
Word and way. Help me remember that no matter what
happens, I'm safe in You. That in You I can find the rest
that heals, refreshes, and rejuvenates. Plant Your wisdom
in my heart, God of all, so that I can sleep in peace with
no cause for fear, knowing You are watching over me,
protecting me. You are guarding my steps, making sure
I'm on the right path.

In You alone can I sleep the sleep of peace. In Jesus'
name I pray, amen.

UNSEEN AND ETERNAL

*So we do not lose heart. Though our outer self is
wasting away, our inner self is being renewed day by
day. For this light momentary affliction is preparing
for us an eternal weight of glory beyond all comparison,
as we look not to the things that are seen but to the things
that are unseen. For the things that are seen are transient,
but the things that are unseen are eternal.*

2 CORINTHIANS 4:16–18 ESV

Lord, I refuse to worry or panic about things over which
I have no control. For I do not want—and was not
designed—to live a life consumed by fretfulness over
every little thing, including my age.

I realize that with each passing day my outer self,
my outer woman, is aging. For that is the way of nature.
Yet the spiritual is a vastly different matter. Although my
outer woman may have a few gray hairs, my inner woman
is being renewed each day. For You are preparing me for
a much grander and more wonderful place.

Thus, I will keep my eyes on the unseen rather than
the seen, knowing that what I can see is fading away,
but what is unseen will last forever. Amen.

Soul to Soul

*I will set My dwelling in and among you, and My soul
shall not despise or reject or separate itself from you. And
I will walk in and with and among you and will be your
God, and you shall be My people. I am the Lord your God,
Who brought you forth out of the land of Egypt, that you
should no more be slaves; and I have broken the bars of
your yoke and made you walk erect [as free men].*

Leviticus 26:11–13 ampc

You and I are linked, Lord, Soul to soul. You have promised
to be with me always, to walk beside me and live within
me, never to hate, reject, or abandon me.

You have brought me so far, Lord, in this journey of
life. From an egg within my mother's womb to my present
self, You have led me to Your love, protection, and joy. You
have brought me out of the darkness and into Your light.
You have made me a free and upright woman, wanting
and loving to be with You and to please You. In You, I
find the peace, the calm, and the delight I desire. Amen.

SLEEP WELL

You, O LORD, are a shield around me; you are my glory, the one who holds my head high. I cried out to the LORD, and he answered me from his holy mountain. . . . I lay down and slept, yet I woke up in safety, for the LORD was watching over me. I am not afraid of ten thousand enemies who surround me on every side. . . . Victory comes from you, O LORD. May you bless your people.

PSALM 3:3–6, 8 NLT

If not for You holding my hand, Lord, I would stumble and fall. If not for Your protection, I would lose courage. Continue, Lord, to be the shield that surrounds me, the One who helps me keep my cool no matter what others say about me.

You, Lord, are the only One I can truly depend on, for You answer me when I call. You sweep onto the scene when I am in trouble. Because I know You will never leave or abandon me, I am able to sleep well at night and arise knowing I'm safe, for my tent is pitched in Your camp. My small hand is held in Your larger one. Because You watch over me, I have nothing to fear. Amen.

RICHNESS IN GOD

God's power is working in us. . . . We serve God
whether people honor us or despise us, whether they
slander us or praise us. We are honest, but they call us
impostors. . . . Our hearts ache, but we always have joy.
We are poor, but we give spiritual riches to others.
We own nothing, and yet we have everything.

2 CORINTHIANS 6:7–8, 10 NLT

I'm not sure people know what to think of me sometimes,
Lord. For even though I seem meek, mild, and gentle to
them, I have such strength in and from You. That's why
I can do the things You have called me to do. So no
matter how I am treated by others, I still look to and serve
You. And I'm good with that. No matter how much my
heart may ache at times, I can always find an abundance
of joy in You. I may not have much materially, but I am
able to give away what I have in spiritual riches. And
although I don't own much of anything, yet in You I
have all I need—and so much more! All praise, glory,
and honor to You!

CALL ON GOD

The Mighty One, God, the Lord, speaks and calls
the earth from the rising of the sun to its setting. . . .
The heavens declare His righteousness (rightness and
justice), for God, He is judge. Selah [pause, and calmly
think of that]! Hear, O My people, and I will speak. . . .
Call on Me in the day of trouble; I will deliver you,
and you shall honor and glorify Me.

PSALM 50:1, 6–7, 15 AMPC

God, You are the One who keeps this world spinning. You
are the Mighty One who can right all wrongs. You can
battle giants, wrestle leviathans, and conquer armies. At
the same time, You are the good and gentle Shepherd who
lovingly calls, guides, and protects Your lambs.

Here I am, Lord. One of Your sheep. I'm in dire
straits. I need You now in all Your power and might to
defend me, deliver me, protect me, pull me up out of
this frenzied fray. Save me from those who have come to
trouble me. Make their hands weak, their words powerless.
And equip me to say what You would have me say and
do what You would have me do to honor You. Amen.

FOUND

*"When he was still a long way off, his father saw
him. His heart pounding, he ran out, embraced him,
and kissed him. The son started his speech: 'Father,
I've sinned against God, I've sinned before you; I don't
deserve to be called your son ever again.' But the father
wasn't listening. He was calling to the servants, 'Quick.
Bring a clean set of clothes and dress him. Put the family
ring on his finger and sandals on his feet.'"*
LUKE 15:20–22 MSG

Thank You, Lord, for always keeping Your eye out for me,
no matter how far I've strayed. You're always opening Your
arms to me, pulling me into Your embrace, kissing me,
loving me. You barely even listen to my sad apology, the
speech I have practiced over and over again, the one in
which I tell You how much I have misstepped. How You
no longer even have to call me Your daughter. Instead,
seeing me back home, once more before You, You are
calling out commands, saying that I should be honored
because I was lost but now am found. Oh, what love You
have for Your children, Father! Amen.

STAND IN AWE

For the word of the LORD is right, and all His work is
trustworthy. He loves righteousness and justice; the earth
is full of the LORD's unfailing love. . . . Let the whole earth
tremble before the LORD; let all the inhabitants of the
world stand in awe of Him. For He spoke, and it came into
being; He commanded, and it came into existence. . . .
The counsel of the LORD stands forever, the plans of
His heart from generation to generation.

PSALM 33:4–5, 8–9, 11 HCSB

I've got no worries today, Lord, because I have Your Word.
And if I have any questions, if I need peace, if I need
help, if I need love, all I need to do is come to You and
ask that You would show me the answers I'm searching
for and provide the calm I crave, the help I need, and
the love I long for.

Lord, before You and Your power, I stand in awe. For
nothing is here that You have not made. You speak, and
things that never existed become reality. You command,
and things just are. Because of You, I am! Amen.

TRUEST FRIEND

There are "friends" who destroy each other, but a
real friend sticks closer than a brother.... "There is
no greater love than to lay down one's life for one's
friends. You are my friends if you do what I command.
I no longer call you slaves, because a master doesn't
confide in his slaves. Now you are my friends."

PROVERBS 18:24; JOHN 15:13–15 NLT

I have many acquaintances, Lord, but I have few close
friends, ones who I know will stick by me through thick
and thin. Yet without a doubt my truest, most loving
friend is You, Lord. Only You loved me so much that You
laid down Your life for me—and that was before I even
came into being! Your great love boggles my mind and
moves my heart.

Yet what I love even more is that You have claimed
me as Your friend—again, before I even knew You. And
all I have to do to honor that friendship is to obey You,
to do what is right in Your eyes. Help me to honor You
in that way every day, Lord, for You are my truest Friend.

Never Alone

And when (if) I go and make ready a place for you,
I will come back again and will take you to Myself,
that where I am you may be also. . . . Where I am going,
you know the way. Thomas said to Him, Lord, we do not
know where You are going, so how can we know the way?
Jesus said to him, I am the Way and the Truth and the
Life; no one comes to the Father except by (through) Me.

John 14:3–6 AMPC

Many times I have felt alone, Lord, as friends and family have drifted in and out of my life, each heading their own way. Yet I know that I am and never will be really alone, for I have and always will have You, my Companion, Guide, Friend, and Brother. You gave Your all so I could be free. And I know, Lord Jesus, that although You have gone ahead to prepare a place for me, You are also within and beside me. How wonderful that because I follow You—the Way, the Truth, and the Life—You and I will be together both now and forever. Amen.

Surprised by Love

God roared in protest, let loose his hurricane anger.
But me he caught—reached all the way from sky to sea;
he pulled me out of that ocean of hate, that enemy chaos,
the void in which I was drowning. They hit me when I was
down, but God stuck by me. He stood me up on a wide-
open field; I stood there saved—surprised to be loved!
2 Samuel 22:16–20 msg

When I am drowning in my sorrows, problems, unanswered questions, worries, and what-ifs, You come along and save me, Lord. Even when others might kick me when I'm down, You are there with me, standing immovable, right by my side.

Thank You, God, for sticking by me. For pulling me up out of the deep waters where I cannot save myself. For getting me out of jams and setting me down in wide-open spaces where I can breathe once more and stand there safe, amazed that You love me like no one else ever could. Amen.

In His Name

*"I tell you the truth, anyone who believes in me will
do the same works I have done, and even greater works,
because I am going to be with the Father. You can ask
for anything in my name, and I will do it, so that the
Son can bring glory to the Father. Yes, ask me for
anything in my name, and I will do it!"*

John 14:12–14 nlt

This promise is so hard to believe, Lord Jesus. That if I have faith in You, I can do the same works here on earth that You have done—or perhaps even greater works! Yet that is the truth You have laid at my door. That is what is written in Your Word.

You continually surprise me. For You, Lord, are always doing the unbelievable, the seemingly impossible. And all You ask of me is to believe, to have faith in who You are and what You can do.

So here I am, Lord, asking something in Your name. And I am believing that, if it's according to Your will, it is something You will do. All so that You can bring glory to our Father! That's something we both can celebrate. In Your name, amen. Amen!

A WALL OF FIRE

The angel who talked with me. . .said to the second angel,
Run, speak to this young man, saying, Jerusalem shall be
inhabited and dwell as villages without walls, because of
the multitude of people and livestock in it. For I, says the
Lord, will be to her a wall of fire round about, and I
will be the glory in the midst of her.

ZECHARIAH 2:3–5 AMPC

Some days, Lord, there are so many troubles in this world
that I feel like what I really need is a wall of fire around
me, a barrier from all that has the potential to harm me.
I need a wall against people, places, and situations that
seem determined to destroy my peace. I need a seawall
to cling to so that I won't be pulled down into the water,
beneath the waves.

Help me to see You as my Protector, Lord. Help me
to know You are there, even though I may not be able to
see You. When I need Your comfort and strength, be that
hedge of protection that will stay in place until I can once
more stand sure and strong upon my own feet. In Jesus'
name I pray, amen.

As Good as Done

A Roman captain came up in a panic and said,
"Master, my servant is sick. He can't walk. He's in
terrible pain." Jesus said, "I'll come and heal him."
"Oh, no," said the captain. "I don't want to put you to
all that trouble. Just give the order and my servant will
be fine. I'm a man who takes orders and gives orders.
I tell one soldier, 'Go,' and he goes; to another, 'Come,'
and he comes; to my slave, 'Do this,' and he does it."

MATTHEW 8:5–9 MSG

Lord, I hate to panic. Yet causes for panic seem to crop up so frequently these days. When some unexpected trouble strikes, uneasiness wells up within me. The next thing I know, my mind is imagining all kinds of wild scenarios. My heart starts beating faster, my breath starts coming more quickly, and there I am—in full-blown panic mode!

So at the first sign of trouble, Lord, prompt my heart and spirit to seek Yours, to tell You what is happening. Then send me a word from You. For I know that as You give a command, it's as good as done. In Your name, amen.

Restored and Complete

God made my life complete when I placed all the pieces before him. When I cleaned up my act, he gave me a fresh start. Indeed, I've kept alert to God's ways; I haven't taken God for granted. Every day I review the ways he works, I try not to miss a trick. I feel put back together, and I'm watching my step. God rewrote the text of my life when I opened the book of my heart to his eyes.

2 Samuel 22:21–25 msg

God, You have known me all of my life. You know when I have fallen apart, when I've brought the pieces of myself before You and allowed You to restore me, to make me the woman You originally created me to be. Then, when I was complete once more, You gave me a fresh start in life. Ever since then, I've looked to You and followed Your way. I've tried not to miss any opportunity You put before me to obey You and keep myself out of trouble. Because of my desire to serve You, to live for You, to lay my heart open before You, You have rewarded me. And all I have left to do is praise Your name! Amen.

Marvelous Believer

Taken aback, Jesus said, "I've yet to come across this kind
of simple trust in Israel, the very people who are supposed
to know all about God and how he works. This man is the
vanguard of many outsiders who will soon be coming from
all directions. . . ." Then Jesus turned to the captain and
said, "Go. What you believed could happen has happened."
At that moment his servant became well.

MATTHEW 8:10–11, 13 MSG

I trust You, Lord, with all things. I have faith that You will
do what You say, that You will come through as promised.
I may not have grown up believing You as I do now, but
having read Your Book and seen Your power at work in
the lives of others, I now know that You are the true
Authority, the Master of all things, the Beginning and
the End, my Creator, Beloved, Healer, and Friend. No
one and nothing compares to You.

And because of my great faith in You, I know that
through You, what I believe can happen will happen. In
Your name, amen.

REMINDERS

The king said to me, "Why are you sad, when you aren't sick? . . ." I was overwhelmed with fear and replied to the king, "May the king live forever! Why should I not be sad when the city where my ancestors are buried lies in ruins and its gates have been destroyed by fire?" Then the king asked me, "What is your request?" So I prayed to the God of heaven and answered the king.

NEHEMIAH 2:2–5 HCSB

Lord, when I am overwhelmed with fear and sadness, remind me who You are. Tell me once more that through You, I can find the courage to do what You prompt me to do. That because You are in my life, I need not be sad. For You can make miracles out of misery and turn troubles into triumph.

Most of all, Lord, remind me of the power of prayer, anytime and anywhere. For prayer is not just for those quiet moments alone when I have time to think things out and find my way into Your presence, but it's also for those times when I need on-the-spot help, when I need to send up a quick arrow prayer to You before I open my mouth. Remind me, Lord, of all the benefits of trusting in You. Amen.

Parting Gifts

"If you love me, obey my commandments. And I will ask the Father, and he will give you another Advocate, who will never leave you." . . . "The Holy Spirit. . .will teach you everything and will remind you of everything I have told you. I am leaving you with a gift—peace of mind and heart. And the peace I give is a gift the world cannot give. So don't be troubled or afraid."

John 14:15–16, 26–27 nlt

Lord, because I love You, my desire is to obey Your commands. Yet I need Your help to obey. That's why I am so grateful You left Your peace of mind and heart for me. And that our Father has gifted me with an Advocate who not only will teach me what I need to know and remind me of all You have told me but also will never leave me.

Both parting gifts are very much needed to keep me on the right track, Lord, to keep me going in Your will and Your way. Thank You for such precious presents. Because of Your peace and Your Spirit, I can rest assured that I need never be troubled or afraid. In Your name I pray, amen.

HEALER OF BROKEN HEARTS

When the righteous cry for help, the Lord hears, and delivers them out of all their distress and troubles. The Lord is close to those who are of a broken heart and saves such as are crushed with sorrow for sin and are humbly and thoroughly penitent. Many evils confront the [consistently] righteous, but the Lord delivers him out of them all. He keeps all his bones; not one of them is broken.

PSALM 34:17–20 AMPC

Lord of the brokenhearted, hear my cry. Mend the wounds that scar my being. Lift me up from the bottom of this pit in which my spirit is mired. Deliver me from all my missteps and mistakes. Bind me back together again.

Lord, You know what has crushed my spirit. You know what has driven me down. You know the darkness that has enveloped me. Yet You are the Lord of light. You hold the answer to my plea. Sun of Righteousness with healing in Your wings, fly close to me. Allow Your rays of light to beam down upon me, to warm me, to lift me up and draw me closer to You, where all is well. Amen.

GOD-GIVEN SPIRIT

God did not give us a spirit of timidity (of cowardice,
of craven and cringing and fawning fear), but [He has
given us a spirit] of power and of love and of calm and well-
balanced mind and discipline and self-control. . . . Guard
and keep [with the greatest care] the precious and excellently
adapted [Truth] which has been entrusted [to you], by the
[help of the] Holy Spirit Who makes His home in us.
2 TIMOTHY 1:7, 14 AMPC

Shaper of beings, please reawaken my spirit. Remind me of who You are and what You've had planned for me since the beginning of time. Take away my cowardice, my fears, those insecurities that keep me from doing the things You'd have me do. Infuse my spirit with Your light so that it will be as originally intended by You, a spirit of power, love, calm, sensibility, discipline, and self-control. Then, through the power of Your Holy Spirit whose home is within me, help me guard the truths You have entrusted to me. In Jesus' name I pray, amen.

LORD OF LIGHT

*You stick by people who stick with you, you're straight
with people who're straight with you, you're good to good
people, you shrewdly work around the bad ones. You take
the side of the down-and-out, but the stuck-up you take
down a peg. Suddenly, GOD, your light floods my path,
GOD drives out the darkness. . . . What a God! His road
stretches straight and smooth. Every GOD-direction is
road-tested. Everyone who runs toward him makes it.*

2 SAMUEL 22:26–29, 31 MSG

Because like attracts like, Light attracts light. That's why
I can connect with You, Lord. For You are close to those
who are close to You. You are honest with those who are
honest with You. You're good to the good. That's why I'm
here, Lord, standing before You. I need the light of Your
being to brighten the darkness in which I find myself,
for I can't find my way around on my own.

Illuminate the shadows with Your lamp, Lord of
light. Flood my pathway with Your being so that I can
find my way out of this murky night. Be my shield, my
refuge, my ally in this life as I seek Your will and way. In
Jesus' name, amen.

No Fear

"Don't be afraid of those who want to kill your body; they cannot touch your soul. Fear only God, who can destroy both soul and body in hell. What is the price of two sparrows—one copper coin? But not a single sparrow can fall to the ground without your Father knowing it. And the very hairs on your head are all numbered. So don't be afraid; you are more valuable to God than a whole flock of sparrows."
MATTHEW 10:28–31 NLT

Invincible Lord, gird my spirit. Give me the courage I need to face each day, each situation, each person I encounter. Remind me that I need not fear bullies who want to harm my body but can't touch my soul. All I need is a healthy fear of You, the almighty Lord, who can kill both my body and my soul.

God of all creation, You have Your eyes on every living thing, even sparrows. Not one can fall to the ground without Your awareness. And just as You take notice of small birds, You are even more attentive to me, knowing and valuing every part of my being. I never need to fear, for I mean more to You than one or even an entire flock of sparrows.

Look Up, Power Up

Lift up your eyes on high and see! Who has created these? He Who brings out their host by number and calls them all by name; through the greatness of His might and because He is strong in power, not one is missing or lacks anything. . . . He gives power to the faint and weary, and to him who has no might He increases strength [causing it to multiply and making it to abound].

Isaiah 40:26, 29 ampc

Lord of creation, it's hard to imagine how You have formed all the stars I see when I look up to the heavens. You bring them out into the night sky, one by one, calling each by name. Because of Your power and might, not one star is missing or lacks anything.

Just as You name and care for Your celestial beings, You name and care for me. And so You are the One I run to for power when I feel done in. You are the One I go to for strength. For You are my God, my Creator, my Sustainer, my Star Namer! Amen.

OPEN DOORS

A wide door for effective ministry has opened for me—
yet many oppose me. . . . Be alert, stand firm in the faith,
act like a man, be strong. Your every action must be
done with love. . . . This greeting is in my own hand—
Paul. . . . The grace of the Lord Jesus be with you.
My love be with all of you in Christ Jesus.
1 CORINTHIANS 16:9, 13–14, 21, 23–24 HCSB

Lord of love, give me the courage I need to do what You call me to do. Help me to keep my eyes open and to stay alert. When a door for ministry opens before me, give me boldness to walk through it. Even though others oppose me, give me the moxie to trust in You.

Help me, Lord Jesus, to stand firm in You, to act like a brave woman and be strong—not just physically but spiritually, mentally, and emotionally. Remind me to act in a loving way in all circumstances.

Most of all, Lord, give me the wisdom to take a personal interest in everything that is of You. And to do so with Your grace and love. In Your sweet name I pray, amen.

RENEWAL

Even youths shall faint and be weary, and [selected] young men shall feebly stumble and fall exhausted; but those who wait for the Lord [who expect, look for, and hope in Him] shall change and renew their strength and power; they shall lift their wings and mount up [close to God] as eagles [mount up to the sun]; they shall run and not be weary, they shall walk and not faint or become tired.

ISAIAH 40:30–31 AMPC

My body is weary, Lord. Gravity pulls on my spirit and soul, casting them down, down, down. So I come to You, exhausted, tired, feeble in every way. And I wait upon You. I expect and look for the relief I will find in Your presence. And as I wait, I find my strength renewed, my power recharged, my hope revitalized. Like an eagle, I lift up my wings and soar close to You.

Because of You who exude strength, power, and life, I am no longer weary. My inner woman rises up in Your presence. I can now run and not tire, walk and not become weary. For You have more than met my expectations, and You are all I ever need, in this world and the next. Amen.

THE TRANSLATING SPIRIT

*The Spirit helps us in our weakness. For we do not
know what to pray for as we ought, but the Spirit himself
intercedes for us with groanings too deep for words. And he
who searches hearts knows what is the mind of the Spirit,
because the Spirit intercedes for the saints according to the
will of God. And we know that for those who love God
all things work together for good, for those who
are called according to his purpose.*

ROMANS 8:26–28 ESV

Holy Spirit, come to me. I don't know what to pray, what
to say. Search my wounded heart. Read the emotions in
my soul, the thoughts in my mind, the conflicts within my
spirit. Take all my outward moans and groans and plead
to God on my behalf, translating and transforming all
I am, feel, and want to say into the proper words for the
Lord's hearing. Above all, reassure me that You will intercede for me, helping my thoughts, words, and actions to
align with my Master's will and way. I know God will work
all things into a plan for good for all. Amen.

Journeying with the Lord

*Whenever the cloud lifted from the Tabernacle,
the people of Israel would set out on their journey,
following it. But if the cloud did not rise, they remained
where they were until it lifted. The cloud of the Lord
hovered over the Tabernacle during the day, and at night
fire glowed inside the cloud so the whole family of Israel
could see it. This continued throughout all their journeys.*

Exodus 40:36–38 nlt

I need clear direction, Lord, just like what You gave the Israelites when they were wandering in the wilderness. Remind me to keep my eye out for You, to look for You day and night. To search for where You may already be and to go where You bid me to go. Help me to be very in tune with Your presence, sensing when You're near and going wherever You lead.

Show me, Lord, where You want me to remain and when You want me to move on. For my true desire is to follow Your will and way—day and night. Through every stage of my journey, be a viable presence, glowing so that I can see You in every circumstance. Amen.

NOTHING BUT PRAISE

Mary said, My soul magnifies and extols the Lord, and
my spirit rejoices in God my Savior. . . . For He Who is
almighty has done great things for me—and holy is His
name [to be venerated in His purity, majesty and glory]! . . .
He has shown strength and made might with His arm;
He has scattered the proud and haughty in and by the
imagination and purpose and designs of their hearts.

LUKE 1:46–47, 49, 51 AMPC

Today, dearest and most magnificent Lord, I come to You with nothing but praise. For You have done so many great things for me. You gave me peace in the midst of hardship. You showered me with calm in times of great stress. You imbued me with strength when I was at my weakest. Time after time, You made the impossible possible.

Almighty Savior, You have rescued me before I even had a chance to call Your name. That is why my spirit is brimming with praise, my eyes gleaming with wonder, my heart soaring above the clouds. You have proved to be the best Life Companion a woman could ever have. Amen.

LEVEL GROUND

Cause me to hear Your loving-kindness in the morning,
for on You do I lean and in You do I trust. Cause me to
know the way wherein I should walk, for I lift up my inner
self to You. Deliver me, O Lord, from my enemies; I flee
to You to hide me. Teach me to do Your will, for You are
my God; let Your good Spirit lead me into a level
country and into the land of uprightness.

PSALM 143:8–10 AMPC

When I rise, Lord, speak to my heart. Tell me how much You love me and long to be kind to me. For I am leaning my entire self upon You, the One I trust above all others. Show me the way that I am to go. Lead me where You would have me walk. For I'm lifting my inner being up to You.

Keep wrongdoers far from my door, Lord. If they do get close, allow me to hide within You, my shield and refuge. With patience, teach me to do what You would have me do, for I long to please You, Lord. Lead me to walk upon level ground where I won't trip, fall, or fail You. In Jesus' name, amen.

GOD'S SERVANT

*Run away from childish indulgence. Run after mature
righteousness—faith, love, peace—joining those who
are in honest and serious prayer before God. Refuse to get
involved in inane discussions; they always end up in fights.
God's servant must not be argumentative, but a gentle
listener and a teacher who keeps cool, working firmly but
patiently with those who refuse to obey. You never know
how or when God might sober them up with a change
of heart and a turning to the truth.*

2 TIMOTHY 2:22–25 MSG

These days it seems so easy to get caught up in things
that are a waste of time. Instead, Lord, I want to pursue
things that are good, such as faith, love, and peace. At the
same time, I want to avoid getting pulled into ridiculous
arguments that can go on and on just to end in conflict.
But to do what's right and avoid what's wrong, Lord, I
need Your help and strength. Make me a gentle listener,
one who pays close attention to the words and needs of
others. And help me keep my cool and my patience with
those who are difficult—for who knows when they may
have a change of mind and an open heart? Amen.

Be Lifted Up

Lift up your heads, O you gates; and be lifted up, you
age-abiding doors, that the King of glory may come in.
Who is the King of glory? The Lord strong and mighty,
the Lord mighty in battle. Lift up your heads, O you gates;
yes, lift them up, you age-abiding doors, that the King of
glory may come in. Who is [He then] this King of glory?
The Lord of hosts, He is the King of glory.

Psalm 24:7–10 ampc

Lord, I have been trying to be my own fortress, refuge,
and strength. But it's not working. So I'm finally coming
to You for help.

Help me, Lord, to open up to You. To allow You to
be my Lord and Master. Help me to allow You to enter
my heart, mind, soul, and spirit.

I have put up so many barriers to You. Although
I seem to say the right words, pray the right prayers,
and read the right books, I still hold back from letting
You have all of me. That stops. Today. In this moment.

Here I am, Lord. I'm lifting up my head, opening
my gates, unbarring my doors so that You, the King of
glory, may come in. Now and forever, amen.

A Shining Light

*Because of and through the heart of tender mercy and
loving-kindness of our God, a Light from on high will dawn
upon us and visit [us] to shine upon and give light to those
who sit in darkness and in the shadow of death, to direct
and guide our feet in a straight line into the way of peace.*

Luke 1:78–79 ampc

In the darkest of times, when sin and evil seemed to rule
the roost, You, Lord, brought a Light into the lives of
Your people. And it was all because of Your tender
mercy and love for them. For me.

This Light You brought to us came down and shined
upon those who were sitting in darkness. This same Light
directed our feet, helping us to walk in a straight line and
into the way of peace. The Light's name was Jesus. And
we need Him now more than ever, Lord.

Make the presence of Your Son very real in our lives.
Prompt us to look up and out for Him, to run to Him when
His light shines upon us, to answer His call. Show us the
way back to His peace. Amen.

A HIDING PLACE

Let everyone who is godly offer prayer to you at a time
when you may be found; surely in the rush of great waters,
they shall not reach him. You are a hiding place for me; you
preserve me from trouble; you surround me with shouts of
deliverance. I will instruct you and teach you in the way
you should go. . . . Many are the sorrows of the wicked, but
steadfast love surrounds the one who trusts in the LORD.

PSALM 32:6–8, 10 ESV

My Deliverer, I come to You once again, knowing my
voice will find Your ear. Hide me, Lord, from any trouble
that may be coming my way. Be my fortress and stronghold. Don't allow the floodwaters to reach me and suck
me under. Fill the air around me with songs of victory.
Most of all, Lord, lead me along the best path for this
life You've laid out for me. Teach me the way that I should
go. And surround me with the light of Your constant
love. In the name of Jesus I pray and trust, amen.

DESERTED PLACES

He touched him, saying, "I am willing; be made clean,"
and immediately the disease left him. Then He ordered
him to tell no one: "But go and show yourself to the priest,
and offer what Moses prescribed for your cleansing as
a testimony to them." But the news about Him spread
even more, and large crowds would come together to
hear Him and to be healed of their sicknesses. Yet He
often withdrew to deserted places and prayed.

LUKE 5:13–16 HCSB

Lord, often I'm so busy working, trying to make ends meet, that I have a hard time getting the rest I need. When I should be taking things easy, I'm volunteering at church, nurturing my family, training my dog, or trying to get some exercise. Next thing I know, I'm so tired that I'm not only crabby but doing none of my tasks well. Help me, Lord, to break the cycle. Help me to follow Your example, to do what You would have me do—to take time to withdraw to an out-of-the-way place, be with You, and pray. In Your name, amen.

MOTHERLY COMFORT

*For thus says the Lord: Behold, I will extend peace to her
like a river, and the glory of the nations like an overflowing
stream; then you will be nursed, you will be carried on her
hip and trotted [lovingly bounced up and down] on her
[God's maternal] knees. As one whom his mother comforts,
so will I comfort you; you shall be comforted in Jerusalem.
When you see this, your heart shall rejoice.*

ISAIAH 66:12–14 AMPC

Oh Lord, I so need Your peace—a ton of it! And I'm also
in need of some tender loving care. I need to be carried for
a while. So I'm coming to You like a babe in arms comes
to her mother. Lift me into Your strong arms. Wipe the
tears from my eyes. Nourish me as only You can. Then
carry me upon Your hip, bounce me on Your knees, and
cover me with the love only You can provide. Allow me
to rest, ever so peacefully, ever so contentedly, in Your
arms until I am strong enough to walk in Your will and
way once more. Amen.

JUST LIKE JESUS

*"Love your enemies, do what is good to those who hate you,
bless those who curse you, pray for those who mistreat you.
If anyone hits you on the cheek, offer the other also. And if
anyone takes away your coat, don't hold back your shirt
either. Give to everyone who asks you, and from one who
takes your things, don't ask for them back. Just as you
want others to do for you, do the same for them."*

LUKE 6:27–31 HCSB

Lord of love, help me to love as You loved. To be kind to
those who don't like me. To bless those who yell at me.
To pray for those who are mean to me.

All these responses You suggest seem to be the opposite of what my flesh wants to do. Thus I need Your Spirit,
Jesus, to help me grow strong enough to offer the other
cheek, to give up my coat and my shirt, and to go above
and beyond the call of duty. In other words, Lord, help
me to become just like You. In Your name I pray, amen.

Unfailing Love

The LORD looks down from heaven and sees the whole human race. From his throne he observes all who live on the earth. He made their hearts, so he understands everything they do. The best-equipped army cannot save a king, nor is great strength enough to save a warrior. Don't count on your warhorse to give you victory—for all its strength, it cannot save you. But the LORD watches over those who fear him, those who rely on his unfailing love.

Psalm 33:13–18 NLT

Lord and King, You understand me and all my fellow humans. After all, You've formed and fashioned each one of our hearts.

Strangely enough, time after time, we depend on other powers to save us—even though You've made it clear no one is more powerful than You. For You are the One who parted a great sea, enabling unarmed slaves to escape a formidable military force. Amid a fierce battle, You made the sun stand still so Your people could have a victory.

You have taught me, Lord, through Your Word and through Your unfailing love, that nothing and no one can save me or give me victory or strength other than You. On You alone I now and forever depend.

GOING DEEP

He said to Simon (Peter), Put out into the deep
[water], and lower your nets for a haul. And Simon (Peter)
answered, Master, we toiled all night [exhaustingly] and
caught nothing [in our nets]. But on the ground of Your
word, I will lower the nets [again]. And when they had
done this, they caught a great number of fish. . . . And they
came and filled both the boats, so that they began to sink.

LUKE 5:4–7 AMPC

There are times, Lord Jesus, when I work and work but
end up having nothing to show for it. And then You come
to me. You see the futility of my labor. And You direct me
to go out even deeper with my work.

I explain that I've labored so hard for so long and
have nothing to prove I've done so. But because You want
me to extend myself one more time, I will do as You ask
on the ground of Your Word. As soon as I obey Your
command, I find myself blessed beyond all belief.

Thank You, Lord, for encouraging me to go deep
and helping me build up even more trust in You. Amen.

HELP AND SHIELD

*Blessed (happy, fortunate, to be envied) is the nation
whose God is the Lord, the people He has chosen as
His heritage. . . . Our inner selves wait [earnestly] for
the Lord; He is our Help and our Shield. For in Him does
our heart rejoice, because we have trusted (relied on and
been confident) in His holy name. Let Your mercy and
loving-kindness, O Lord, be upon us, in proportion
to our waiting and hoping for You.*

PSALM 33:12, 20–22 AMPC

When I put my hope in people, Lord, I end up disappointed. And that's when I remember where I'm *supposed* to put my hope—in You. You are the One, Lord, who always keeps His promises. You are the One who always does as He says. So I'm putting my hope—*all* my hope—in You. For You are there to help when I need it. And You continually shield me from dangers seen and unseen.

Because of Your assurance that You will always be by my side, I can have peace. I can rejoice in Your persistent presence. Above all, I can trust and expect that Your mercy, love, and kindness are coming my way. In Jesus' name, amen.

The Driver's Seat

Then he told them what they could expect for themselves:
"Anyone who intends to come with me has to let me lead.
You're not in the driver's seat—I am. Don't run from
suffering; embrace it. Follow me and I'll show you how.
Self-help is no help at all. Self-sacrifice is the way, my way,
to finding yourself, your true self. What good would it do
to get everything you want and lose you, the real you?"

Luke 9:23–25 msg

So many times, Lord, I find I've taken the wheel of my life into my own hands, clutching the steering wheel with a white-knuckled grip. And because *I'm* the one in the driver's seat, I'm the one steering the car off the road.

So, Lord, I'm turning the wheel over to You. You are now in the driver's seat. No matter what happens, I'm keeping to the passenger side in this vehicle of life. I'm sacrificing all, putting all into Your steady hands because I know that's the only way I will discover who I truly am and what You have designed me to be and do. In Your name I ride and pray, amen.

HEART AND SOUL

"The LORD will stay with you as long as you stay with
him! Whenever you seek him, you will find him." ...
They entered into a covenant to seek the LORD, the God
of their ancestors, with all their heart and soul. ...
All in Judah were happy about this covenant, for they
had entered into it with all their heart. They earnestly
sought after God, and they found him. And the LORD
gave them rest from their enemies on every side.

2 CHRONICLES 15:2, 12, 15 NLT

Sometimes, Lord, I feel as if I'm in a fog, just going through the motions. I need a rejuvenation, a resurgence of energy in my heart and soul. So I come to You, Lord. I'm coming to seek You with my whole heart, mind, spirit, soul, and strength. I'm going to look for You earnestly within and without. Because once I do, once I commit myself to finding You, I will find You. And then I will be able to enter into real peace and rest. In Jesus' name, amen.

JUST ASK

So I say to you, Ask and keep on asking and it shall be given
you; seek and keep on seeking and you shall find; knock
and keep on knocking and the door shall be opened to you.
For everyone who asks and keeps on asking receives; and
he who seeks and keeps on seeking finds; and to him who
knocks and keeps on knocking, the door shall be opened.

LUKE 11:9–10 AMPC

My prayer life sometimes hits a slump, Lord. That's
when I come to You with a more persistent, determined,
and dedicated mindset. Going forward, when I request
something that is within Your will, I'm going to ask and
keep on asking. I'm going to seek and keep on seeking.
I'm going to knock and keep on knocking. Because You
have promised that when I'm persistent in prayer and ask
something of You, I will receive it. If I seek, I'll find. And
if I knock, a door will be opened to me. As I ASK—Ask,
Seek, Knock—our good Father will hear and move. To
and for His glory! Amen.

FOR SUCH A TIME

Then Mordecai told them to return this answer to Esther,
Do not flatter yourself that you shall escape in the king's
palace any more than all the other Jews. For if you keep
silent at this time, relief and deliverance shall arise for the
Jews from elsewhere, but you and your father's house will
perish. And who knows but that you have come to the
kingdom for such a time as this and for this very occasion?
ESTHER 4:13–14 AMPC

I'm not sure, Lord, why I'm in the kingdom at this particular time and in this particular place. What would You have me do that I'm not already doing? What would You have me say to further Your kingdom? What particular talents or skills or experiences have You given me that I am to use in this time and place?

I am Your vessel, Lord, to do as You please. So please show me, Lord, the mission You would have me undertake. Then stand with me so that I will have the strength, peace, and determination to do as You bid. In Jesus' name I pray, amen.

Soaking Up

*"What I'm trying to do here is get you to relax,
not be so preoccupied with getting so you can respond
to God's giving. People who don't know God and the
way he works fuss over these things, but you know both
God and how he works. Steep yourself in God-reality,
God-initiative, God-provisions. You'll find all your
everyday human concerns will be met. Don't be afraid
of missing out. You're my dearest friends! The Father
wants to give you the very kingdom itself."*

Luke 12:29–32 msg

These days I am anything but relaxed, Lord. So here I am
before You, looking for a word of calm and wisdom. Help
me not to be so intent on getting things that I don't see
what You're giving, what You're doing in this time. Help
me to soak up Your reality, Your plans, Your provisions.
Give me the faith to rely on You for all my everyday needs,
knowing You will more than meet them. And help me
not to be envious of what others have but grateful for all
You have given me as Your daughter and an heir of Your
magnificent kingdom. Amen.

Triumph in Yahweh

*Though the fig tree does not bud and there is no fruit
on the vines, though the olive crop fails and the fields
produce no food, though there are no sheep in the pen
and no cattle in the stalls, yet I will triumph in Yahweh;
I will rejoice in the God of my salvation! Yahweh my
Lord is my strength; He makes my feet like those of a
deer and enables me to walk on mountain heights!*

Habakkuk 3:17–19 HCSB

No matter how bad things may look in this world, Lord, remind me of who You are and what You do. Even if crops fail, my belly rumbles in hunger, and I run out of things to eat, I will still sing Your praises. No matter what happens or doesn't happen, I will still have joy in You, the One who has saved me! For You are the One who nourishes my spirit. You are the One who feeds my soul. You are the God who gives me the strength I need to rise up, to take that higher road, to walk in Your will and according to Your way. Amen.

FORGIVENESS

Pay attention and always be on your guard [looking out for one another]. If your brother sins (misses the mark), solemnly tell him so and reprove him, and if he repents (feels sorry for having sinned), forgive him. And even if he sins against you seven times in a day, and turns to you seven times and says, I repent [I am sorry], you must forgive him (give up resentment and consider the offense as recalled and annulled).

Luke 17:3–4 ampc

There are times, Lord, when my capacity to forgive others seems limited. Yet that is what You call me to do—to forgive as You have forgiven me. And to do so every time that person wrongs me, every time they say, "I'm sorry," no matter how often and no matter what the offense!

Yet although unlimited forgiveness seems difficult, I have to remember how many times You have forgiven me. And every time I have said and meant the words "I'm sorry, Lord," You have accepted my apology. You have forgiven me, no matter what I've done or how often. With those thoughts in mind, Lord, I *will* find a way to do as You ask, and do so quickly. With Jesus' help and in His name I *will* forgive. Amen.

AGREE WITH GOD

*Acquaint now yourself with Him [agree with God
and show yourself to be conformed to His will] and be at
peace; by that [you shall prosper and great] good shall
come to you. Receive, I pray you, the law and instruction
from His mouth and lay up His words in your heart.
If you return to the Almighty. . .and make the Almighty
your gold and [the Lord] your precious silver treasure,
then you will have delight in the Almighty.*

JOB 22:21–23, 25–26 AMPC

When I'm not feeling the peace of Your presence, Lord,
I find myself wondering how I may have walked out of
Your will. I think back over what has been happening in
my life and what I've been doing. I enter into Your Word
and look for where I may have made a mistake. And I
pray, asking You to show me what instruction I've sloughed
off, where I've gone my way instead of Yours. So here I
am, Lord. Reveal to me where I may have faltered in my
walk with You. Show me where I may have gotten off track,
and lead me back to You. In Jesus' name, amen.

Don't Give Up

[Jesus] told them a parable to the effect that they ought always to pray and not to turn coward (faint, lose heart, and give up). . . . The Lord said, Listen to what the unjust judge says! And will not [our just] God defend and protect and avenge His elect (His chosen ones), who cry to Him day and night? Will He defer them and delay help on their behalf?

LUKE 18:1, 6–7 AMPC

This story about the widow who wanted justice is amazing, Lord Jesus. The fact that she kept going back to the judge, one who neither respected nor feared God, is admirable. Although the judge kept refusing to help her, because she was so persistent, he finally gave in to her demands.

I'm so grateful to know, Lord, that God is even more willing to work His justice when we cry to Him day and night, letting Him know what's happening, letting Him know how heavy our hearts are.

I cry out to You today, Lord, asking for justice in this life, this country, this world. You see and know what's happening. Work Your way among Your people, Lord, so that Your will is done and justice and peace reign. Amen.

ACCEPTANCE

He sat [down] among the ashes. Then his wife said to him,
Do you still hold fast your blameless uprightness? Renounce
God and die! But he said to her, You speak as one of the
impious and foolish women would speak. What? Shall we
accept [only] good at the hand of God and shall we not
accept [also] misfortune and what is of a bad nature?
In [spite of] all this, Job did not sin with his lips.

JOB 2:8–10 AMPC

I understand, Lord, that sometimes things that aren't so good will come my way. Times of testing and times of trial. Give me a stout heart so that I will be able to withstand whatever happens in my life. Help me to remember that there will be times I will need to step up to the plate, to have the faith needed to go the distance with You, to learn what You want me to do, to find Your will and way. Help me, Lord, to accept the bad just as easily as I accept the good. For You will turn everything that comes my way to my good in its own time. Amen.

That Deep Connection

"I am the vine; you are the branches. The one who remains in Me and I in him produces much fruit, because you can do nothing without Me. If anyone does not remain in Me, he is thrown aside like a branch and he withers. They gather them, throw them into the fire, and they are burned. If you remain in Me and My words remain in you, ask whatever you want and it will be done for you."

John 15:5–7 hcsb

I can do nothing without You, Lord. I cannot breathe, eat, sleep, work, play, craft, laugh, or cry without You in my life, walking with me every step of the way. So help me to keep a deep connection with You all day long, Lord. Show me how to make sure that I remain in You, that I maintain a strong link to You, heart to heart, mind to mind, spirit to Spirit. Throughout my day, Lord, cause me to stop in my tracks and focus on You, seeking Your face, feeling Your presence, in tune with Your intentions every step of the way. In Your precious name I pray, amen.

ALL THE DIFFERENCE

Caleb quieted the people before Moses, and said, Let us go up at once and possess it; we are well able to conquer it. But his fellow scouts said, We are not able to go up against the people [of Canaan], for they are stronger than we are. . . . There we saw the Nephilim [or giants]. . .and we were in our own sight as grasshoppers, and so we were in their sight.
NUMBERS 13:30–31, 33 AMPC

I want to have the faith of Caleb, Lord. I want that surefire confidence in You that he displayed when he came back from checking out the Promised Land. For Caleb was certain Your people could easily conquer the land. But his fellow spies had a different story. They just saw the strength of the Canaanites and the height of the Nephilim. Those ten other spies were so frightened, their vision of themselves was altered. Instead of seeing themselves as Your people, they saw themselves as measly grasshoppers, sure to get squashed!

Yet Caleb saw You as You are—almighty! Instead of thinking his obstacles were bigger than You, he knew You were bigger than any barrier he'd ever face. And that made all the difference! Amen.

THE WELCOME COMFORTER

If I do not go away, the Comforter (Counselor,
Helper, Advocate, Intercessor, Strengthener, Standby)
will not come to you [into close fellowship with you];
but if I go away, I will send Him to you [to be in close
fellowship with you]. . . . He will guide you into all the
Truth (the whole, full Truth). For He will not speak
His own message [on His own authority]; but He
will tell whatever He hears [from the Father].

John 16:7, 13 ampc

Amazingly enough, Holy Spirit, all the things You represent are all the things I need. Desperately. To have any peace in this world, I need Your comfort. To make wise decisions, I need Your counsel. Because I am just a human, I need Your help. Because I sometimes feel all alone, I need You to be my Advocate. When I can only cry or groan in prayer, I need You to intercede on my behalf with God. When I feel weak and tired, I need Your strength. And because God only knows when You'll be needed by me, I deeply appreciate that You are my Standby. Because of all these things, because of who You are, I welcome You into my heart—now and forever. Amen.

Follow Fully

Because all those men who have seen My glory and My [miraculous] signs which I performed in Egypt and in the wilderness, yet have tested and proved Me these ten times and have not heeded My voice, surely they shall not see the land which I swore to give to their fathers. . . . But My servant Caleb, because he has a different spirit and has followed Me fully, I will bring into the land into which he went.

Numbers 14:22–24 ampc

Lord, unbelievers tend to think I'm naive or on a fantasy trip because I follow You. But I have read of Your works. I have felt Your presence. And You are the One I believe in as my God and Savior. There is no doubt in my mind that You are the real deal. Thus, Lord, I will heed Your voice. I want to follow You fully, continually seeking Your face, sensing Your power, watching You work in the lives of others, and knowing in my heart that You are the God of all. When the time is right, Lord, I know You will bring me into the promised land You have prepared for me. Amen.

"Peace Be with You"

*The disciples were meeting behind locked doors because
they were afraid of the Jewish leaders. Suddenly, Jesus
was standing there among them! "Peace be with you,"
he said. As he spoke, he showed them the wounds in his
hands and his side. They were filled with joy when they
saw the Lord! Again he said, "Peace be with you. As
the Father has sent me, so I am sending you." Then he
breathed on them and said, "Receive the Holy Spirit."*

John 20:19–22 nlt

When I am cowering in fear, Lord, come. Come through
whatever doors I have barricaded myself behind. Make
Your presence known. Stand here before me and say those
precious words, "Peace be with you."

Remind me who You are—my rock, my foundation,
my fortress, my strength, my song. Tell me again how You
have conquered this world. Be the light that breaks up this
darkness in which I find myself. Fill my heart with joy as
I feel Your presence, bask in Your calm, and absorb Your
light. Repeat Your words of peace, then breathe on me
the breath of God. Make me new as I look to You. Amen.

YEARNING FOR LEARNING

Ezra went up from Babylon. He was a skilled scribe in the
five books of Moses. . . . And the king granted him all he
asked, for the hand of the Lord his God was upon him. . . .
Upon him was the good hand of his God. For Ezra had
prepared and set his heart to seek the Law of the Lord [to
inquire for it and of it, to require and yearn for it], and to
do and teach in Israel its statutes and its ordinances.

EZRA 7:6, 9–10 AMPC

This Christian life is not all about You doing things for me,
Lord. It's about pursuing You, yearning for You, serving
You, setting my heart to seek Your face, know Your voice,
learn Your will, follow Your way. Help me to prepare myself
to pray to You. Prompt me to look into Your Word, study
it, and apply it to my life. Place Your hand upon me so that
I can do all You would have me do, be all You would have
me be, and understand all You would have me understand.
May I yearn daily for all You would reveal to me in Your
Word. In Jesus' name, amen.

BLESSED WITHOUT SEEING

The doors were locked; but suddenly, as before,
Jesus was standing among them. "Peace be with you,"
he said. Then he said to Thomas, "Put your finger here,
and look at my hands. Put your hand into the wound in
my side. Don't be faithless any longer. Believe!" "My Lord
and my God!" Thomas exclaimed. Then Jesus told him,
"You believe because you have seen me. Blessed are
those who believe without seeing me."

JOHN 20:26–29 NLT

I've never physically seen You, Lord. But that doesn't keep me from believing in You.

From reading Your Word and feeling the peace of Your Spirit and the joy of Your presence, I know You are my Lord. I know all the things written about You are true. For no one else can get through my frazzled nerves and touch my heart. No one else can bring me the comfort that Your peace affords. No one else can show me the way that makes this journey so wonderful. No one else has watched over me, protected me, and loved me as You have.

Yes, even without seeing You, I am blessed. For all I need, desire, and hope for I find in You. Amen.

The Lifeguard

You are my strength; I wait for you to rescue me,
for you, O God, are my fortress. In his unfailing love,
my God will stand with me. . . . I will sing about your
power. Each morning I will sing with joy about your
unfailing love. For you have been my refuge, a place of
safety when I am in distress. O my Strength, to you
I sing praises, for you, O God, are my refuge.
Psalm 59:9–10, 16–17 nlt

In this crazy world, Lord, I've seen people running around in circles. But I don't take that route. When things are strange and scary, I wait for You to save me. For You are the strength I need. You are the safe place in this increasingly dangerous world. You are the walls I can hide behind.

Because You love me, I know You will stand with me. That's why, when I'm in distress, when I feel like I'm drowning, I look for Your hand to lift me up out of the crashing and crushing waves. You are the Lifeguard I have learned to recognize, rely on, and rest in.

My Champion, my Companion, my Strength—for all that You are, I praise You. Amen.

THE UNTORN NET

He called out, "Fellows, have you caught any fish?"
"No," they replied. Then he said, "Throw out your net
on the right-hand side of the boat, and you'll get some!"
So they did, and they couldn't haul in the net because
there were so many fish in it. Then the disciple Jesus
loved said to Peter, "It's the Lord!" . . . There were
153 large fish, and yet the net hadn't torn.
JOHN 21:5–7, 11 NLT

When I'm discouraged, when I'm worried, when I'm wondering what my next move should be, I hear Your voice calling out to me from the shore. You question me. After I answer, You advise me. Then I follow Your direction, obey Your command. And as soon as I do, as soon as I begin working where You are already abiding, I find myself blessed beyond belief. I am living amid the miracle.

Thank You, Lord Jesus, for paying close attention to every part of my life, every line of my script, every thought in my mind. Thank You for blessing me beyond compare. Thank You for being my miracle. Amen.

God's Way and Word

"As the rain and the snow come down from heaven and do not return there but water the earth, making it bring forth and sprout, giving seed to the sower and bread to the eater, so shall my word be that goes out from my mouth; it shall not return to me empty, but it shall accomplish that which I purpose, and shall succeed in the thing for which I sent it."

<small>ISAIAH 55:10–11 ESV</small>

The power of Your Word is amazing, Lord. From the very beginning, when there was nothing but chaos, You brooded over an earth that had no form. Your Spirit was moving, hovering over the great waters, the deep darkness. And then You said, "Let there be light!" and everything changed. You began making order of the chaos. That is the power of Your Word.

What You say, Lord, changes worlds within and without. You speak and things that had no form suddenly exist. Speak Your Word over me, Lord. Allow it to perform its work. Have Your Word accomplish Your will and purpose as it hovers above me, washes over me, transforms me for You. In Jesus' name I pray, amen.

The Power of Prayer

While Peter was in prison, the church prayed very earnestly for him. The night before Peter was to be placed on trial, he was asleep, fastened with two chains between two soldiers. Others stood guard at the prison gate. Suddenly, there was a bright light in the cell, and an angel of the Lord stood before Peter. The angel struck him on the side to awaken him and said, "Quick! Get up!" And the chains fell off his wrists.

ACTS 12:5–7 NLT

The power of prayer is amazing, Lord. Yet so often I seem to use it as a last resort. I put it to work only when I've exhausted all other ways of finding a solution to a problem for myself or others. Help me change that up, Lord. Show me how to pray as a first remedy for others with all my heart, mind, spirit, and soul and to be persistent and consistent in those prayers.

And if I am the subject of the prayers of others, Lord, help me to stay calm, knowing You're already sending an angel my way to awaken me, give me direction, and free me from whatever is holding me captive. And You will receive all the praise! Amen.

An Angel ahead of Me

Go to my country and to my relatives and take a wife
for my son Isaac. . . . The Lord, the God of heaven,
Who took me from my father's house, from the land
of my family and my birth, Who spoke to me and
swore to me, saying, To your offspring I will give
this land—He will send His Angel before you,
and you will take a wife from there for my son.
Genesis 24:4, 7 ampc

On every mission You send me, Lord, remind me of who I am and who You are.

I am Your servant, one who looks to obey You in every way. I am one who believes in Your Word, who knows that what You say will come to pass. I understand that what You promise will become reality.

I believe that when You send me on a mission for You, You will send Your Angel ahead of me. As a result, I will make no journey alone but will be guided by You and following the path of Your angelic Scout. That's what will make this life journey with You a success. Amen.

Peace of Mind

When they had passed through the first guard and the
second, they came to the iron gate which leads into the city.
Of its own accord [the gate] swung open, and they went
out and passed on through one street; and at once the angel
left him. Then Peter came to himself and said, Now I really
know and am sure that the Lord has sent His angel and
delivered me from the hand of Herod and from all that
the Jewish people were expecting [to do to me].

Acts 12:10–11 AMPC

There are times, Lord, when it feels as if the whole world is against me. Those are the times I need to stop and remember who You are.

You, Lord, are the One who easily thwarts the evil plans of others. You are the One who sends angels to deliver Your people. You are the One whose "power no foe can withstand" (Psalm 91:1 AMPC)!

Help me keep all that in mind, Lord, when the going gets tough. Help me to remember that You are on my side and nothing can keep You from saving me, delivering me, helping me, loving me. You, Lord, are my peace of mind. Amen.

Before We're
Finished Praying

*"When I came to the spring, I prayed this prayer:
'O Lord, God of my master, Abraham, please give
me success on this mission. See, I am standing here beside
this spring. This is my request. . . .' Before I had finished
praying in my heart, I saw Rebekah coming out with her
water jug on her shoulder. . . . Then I bowed low and
worshiped the Lord. I praised the Lord, the God of
my master, Abraham, because he had led me."*

Genesis 24:42–43, 45, 48 NLT

Lord, I stand amazed that You are so interested in and concerned with the affairs of Your praying people. When we plead for success, when we ask You to see where we are standing on this mortal coil, when we give You our specific request, we soon realize that before we are even done praying in our heart of hearts, You are already providing an answer to our prayer. You have already paved the way ahead for our footsteps. You have already planned for our plans.

That is why I bow and worship You in this moment, praising You for leading me to where You would have me go! Amen.

MIRACLE MOMENTS

She recognized Peter's voice, and because of her joy,
she did not open the gate but ran in and announced that
Peter was standing at the gateway. . . . Peter, however,
kept on knocking, and when they opened the door and
saw him, they were astounded. Motioning to them with
his hand to be silent, he explained to them how the Lord
had brought him out of the prison. "Report these
things to James and the brothers," he said.

ACTS 12:14, 16–17 HCSB

You, Lord, have wrought so many miracles in my life. You have delivered me time after time from perilous situations—and who knows how many times You have saved me from unseen dangers? The point is, Lord, that You are continually astounding me with miracle moments.

Show me, Lord, how to share those miracle moments with others. Give me the courage to share every amazing detail of what You have done for me time and time again and to ask others to share their own stories so that all—believers and yet-to-become believers—can learn who You are and how You love and live for Your people. Amen.

Do Not Delay

"Will you or won't you show unfailing love and faithfulness
to my master? Please tell me yes or no, and then I'll know
what to do next." Then Laban and Bethuel replied, "The
Lord has obviously brought you here, so there is nothing
we can say." . . . "But we want Rebekah to stay with us at
least ten days," her brother and mother said. . . . But he
said, "Don't delay me. The Lord has made my mission
successful; now send me back so I can return to my master."

Genesis 24:49–50, 55–56 nlt

When things line up for us amazingly well in certain situations, Lord, we can take it as fact that You have played a big part in it. So when it is clear that any mission for You has been successful, Lord, help me not to remain in neutral but to find a way to move ahead. Give me the strength to continue walking my way back to You. You alone are the One I wait on; You alone I serve. I want to stick to Your schedule. Help me not to tarry nor to run ahead, but to walk in time with Your rhythm of peace and grace. Amen.

SHAKING OFF THE DUST

So the Word of the Lord. . .spread throughout the whole
region. But the Jews stirred up the devout women of high
rank and the outstanding men of the town, and instigated
persecution against Paul and Barnabas and drove them
out of their boundaries. But [the apostles] shook off the
dust from their feet against them and went to Iconium.
And the disciples were continually filled [throughout
their souls] with joy and the Holy Spirit.
ACTS 13:49–52 AMPC

When it comes to spreading Your Word, Lord, I need Your
help. I pray for Your courage to speak out to all people, no
matter their race, creed, color, rank, or wealth. I need Your
strength to stay standing once I've taken up Your position.
I need Your direction as to where to go and how long to
stay. But most of all, Lord, I need Your peace.

When others reject Your Word and reject me as Your
servant, help me not to cower or cry or cringe. Give me
the calm I need to simply shake the dust off my feet and
continue on to the next place You send me. For as I do
so, I know I will be filled to the brim with Your Spirit and
Your joy. In Jesus' name, amen.

MENDED HEARTS

Isaac had returned from going to the well Beer-lahai-roi
[A well to the Living One Who sees me]. . . . Isaac went
out to meditate and bow down [in prayer] in the open
country. . . . Rebekah looked up, and when she saw Isaac,
she dismounted from the camel. . . . Isaac brought her into
his mother Sarah's tent, and he took Rebekah and she
became his wife, and he loved her; thus Isaac was
comforted after his mother's death.

GENESIS 24:62–64, 67 AMPC

Beloved Lord, You continually have Your eye upon me, watching me, providing for me. You, the Living One Who Sees, know what I need. You mend my heart, heal my hurts, and bring me treasures beyond compare.

When my heart is lonely or even a bit empty, Lord, help to heal my wound. Send me just what I need to return to hope, joy, and peace. Ease the ache caused by a grievous sorrow.

You who know me so well, give me the comfort I need, supply the love I lack, and fill the emptiness within so that I may continue to do Your will and walk in Your way. Amen.

Opened Doors

As Paul and Silas were praying and singing hymns of praise to God, and the [other] prisoners were listening to them, suddenly there was a great earthquake, so that the very foundations of the prison were shaken; and at once all the doors were opened and everyone's shackles were unfastened. . . . Then [the jailer] called for lights and rushed in, and trembling and terrified he fell down before Paul and Silas.

Acts 16:25–26, 29 ampc

Prayer and praise are two immensely powerful forces that You have put into my heart and hands, Lord. And the wonder of it is that I need nothing but my own mind to utilize them. Yet still at times I seem reluctant to use these gifts. Help me reverse that course, Lord.

Teach me, God, how to use these forces well. Help me practice prayer and praise. Lead me to a psalm or a hymn I can pray and sing. Help me to shake up my life by implementing the power of Your Word. Help me to open doors for You to work in my life and the lives of others. All in the power of Jesus' name. Amen.

HOLY RELIANCE

May the Lord answer you in the day of trouble! May the
name of the God of Jacob protect you! May he send you
help from the sanctuary and give you support from Zion!
May he remember all your offerings and regard with favor
your burnt sacrifices! May he grant you your heart's desire
and fulfill all your plans! May we shout for joy over your
salvation, and in the name of our God set up our banners!
PSALM 20:1–5 ESV

Lord, You know what has been happening in my life. You
have seen my trials and troubles. Yet I will not fear. Nor will
I panic. For when I cry out to You, I know You will hear
my voice. When I'm in a vulnerable position, I can rely on
You to protect me, to surround me with Your presence.
And You not only will send me help but will grant my
heart's desires and fulfill all my dreams and longings. For
You alone are my joy, my hope, and my Deliverer. You are
my praise at all times and in all ways. Amen.

In Him We Live

"He is the God who made the world and everything
in it. . . . Human hands can't serve his needs—for he has
no needs. He himself gives life and breath to everything,
and he satisfies every need. . . . His purpose was for the
nations to seek after God. . .though he is not far from
any one of us. For in him we live and move and exist."

ACTS 17:24–25, 27–28 NLT

Every morning when I awaken, Lord, I think of You. I wonder at what You have created—myself, my loved ones, and all the nature that surrounds me. I consider what I can do for You, what You might need. And then I remember who You are—the One who has no needs. For You are the One who gives life and breath to everyone.

You, Lord, are the One who supplies and satisfies the needs of everyone and everything. My only true purpose and goal is to seek after You, even though I feel and know You are within, behind, above, beside, and before me as I walk this path and keep to Your way—this day and all the days to come. Amen.

Tears Wiped Away

*He will swallow up death [in victory; He will
abolish death forever]. And the Lord God will
wipe away tears from all faces; and the reproach of
His people He will take away from off all the earth;
for the Lord has spoken it. It shall be said in that day,
Behold our God upon Whom we have waited and hoped,
that He might save us! This is the Lord, we have waited
for Him; we will be glad and rejoice in His salvation.*

Isaiah 25:8–9 ampc

Just when I'm about to give up, just as I'm ready to cry,
just when I feel I cannot go on for the road is too hard and
hazardous, I remember You and Your promises, Lord. For
You have defeated death. You have paved a way for me to
go directly to Father God, to seek His face, to ask for His
help. You have torn down all the barriers separating me
from the Lord God of the universe so that I can find peace,
joy, and confidence in this life and beyond.

So, Lord, help me give up today's burdens and take
up tomorrow's hope. Wipe away my tears and prompt me
to simply rejoice in what You have done in and through
me. Amen.

IN A NIGHT VISION

And one night the Lord said to Paul in a vision,
Have no fear, but speak and do not keep silent; for I
am with you, and no man shall assault you to harm you,
for I have many people in this city. So he settled down
among them for a year and six months, teaching the
Word of God [concerning the attainment through
Christ of eternal salvation in the kingdom of God].

ACTS 18:9–11 AMPC

Speak to me, Lord. Come to me in a dream or vision. Tell me what You would have me know. Advise me on where You would have me go. Take away my fears when I find myself among strangers. Give me the words You would have me speak.

Above all things, Lord, be close to me as I serve You. Protect me from those who would wish me harm. And finally, Lord, give me Your peace as I settle down into You, determining to make my goal to win the souls of others—for You and Your glory. In Jesus' name I pray, amen.

LESSONS FOR HOPE

Whatever was written in the past was written for our instruction, so that we may have hope through endurance and through the encouragement from the Scriptures. . . . Isaiah says: The root of Jesse will appear, the One who rises to rule the Gentiles; the Gentiles will hope in Him. Now may the God of hope fill you with all joy and peace as you believe in Him so that you may overflow with hope by the power of the Holy Spirit.

ROMANS 15:4, 12–13 HCSB

As I read and study the stories of old, Lord, I find myself in some of the Old Testament characters. Your scripture stories give me hope that all will be well. They remind me that miracles do exist. They teach me lessons others had to learn the hard way. They give me the strength and energy to endure when I otherwise may have given up.

Continue to teach me through Your Word, Lord. Help me to sink my teeth into stories that I need to hear. And as I continue to seek You and Your purpose for me, continue to fill me with joy and peace as I overflow with the hope brought to me and working through me by Your Spirit. Amen.

The Way Out

Now I know that the Lord saves His anointed;
He will answer him from His holy heaven with the saving
strength of His right hand. Some trust in and boast of
chariots and some of horses, but we will trust in and boast
of the name of the Lord our God. They are bowed down
and fallen, but we are risen and stand upright.

PSALM 20:6–8 AMPC

When I am weak, worried, and woeful, I come to You, Lord, crying for help, relief, and wisdom. Show me the way out of my troubles. Save me for Your name's sake, for Your glory. Answer me by filling me with Your supernatural strength. For I am not trusting in my fellow humans, nor their devices of defense. Instead, I am trusting in You alone to show me the path I am to take, to give me the words I am to speak, to keep me standing on my feet. And, Lord, as I trust in You, I will boast about You to those who do not know You, praying they will one day see Your light. In Jesus' name, amen.

Take Heart

"I urge you to take heart. . . . For this very night there stood before me an angel of the God to whom I belong and whom I worship, and he said, 'Do not be afraid, Paul; you must stand before Caesar. And behold, God has granted you all those who sail with you.' So take heart, men, for I have faith in God that it will be exactly as I have been told."

ACTS 27:22–25 ESV

When caught in a storm, Lord, whether within or without, I open myself to You. Your voice and Your words give me courage, and I am heartened by Your angels, my ears ringing with the message they bring from You. They tell me not to be afraid. That the plan You have for me is being played out. That You will continue to protect me and those who walk this road with me. And because I have faith in You, the one God I love and worship, I know You will stand by Your words, that what You have told me will be so, and I will be saved. In Jesus' name, amen.

A God of His Word

Balaam took up his [figurative] discourse and said:
Rise up, Balak, and hear; listen [closely] to me, son of
Zippor. God is not a man, that He should tell or act a lie,
neither the son of man, that He should feel repentance or
compunction [for what He has promised]. Has He said and
shall He not do it? Or has He spoken and shall He not make
it good? You see, I have received His command to bless Israel.
He has blessed, and I cannot reverse or qualify it.

NUMBERS 23:18–20 AMPC

Lord, You are not like a human being, one whose words may be false. No. You are the Lord who speaks neither myths nor lies. You always tell me the truth. And You always come through on Your promises. What You say You mean. What You vow to do You will do. What You command is carried out.

I never need to worry, for You promise that You will love, protect, provide for, and bless all those who have faith in You. And that's all I need to know to have Your peace now and forever. Amen.

New Things
out of Nothing

Abraham believed in the God who brings the dead back to life and who creates new things out of nothing. Even when there was no reason for hope, Abraham kept hoping— believing that he would become the father of many nations. For God had said to him, "That's how many descendants you will have!" And Abraham's faith did not weaken, even though, at about 100 years of age, he figured his body was as good as dead—and so was Sarah's womb.

Romans 4:17–19 nlt

Lord, help me to believe in You and the promises You have made even if they look like an impossible task. Help me to keep on trusting You, to keep on hoping, to keep on believing even when there is no reason for hope. Strengthen my faith; don't allow it to weaken no matter how desperate the situation looks. For I know that You can raise people from the dead, make the sun stand still, allow a donkey to talk, and give an old couple a newborn babe to hold in their arms. Remind me that You hold all the power to make all Your promises a reality. In Jesus' name, amen.

WINGS OF REFUGE

"Why are you so kind to notice me. . . ?" Boaz answered her,
"Everything you have done for your mother-in-law since
your husband's death has been fully reported to me: how
you left your father and mother and the land of your birth,
and how you came to a people you didn't previously know.
May the LORD reward you for what you have done, and
may you receive a full reward from the LORD God of Israel,
under whose wings you have come for refuge."
RUTH 2:10–12 HCSB

Give me the courage, Lord, to step out of my comfort
zone and stick with those I love—no matter what I need
to do or how far I have to journey. Give me the strength
to walk on and to commit to helping those who are alone
and need a companion to come alongside them. Give me
wisdom to know how to support those who are down-and-
out, bitter, or full of sorrow. Give me the persistence to
continue on, knowing that someday You will reward me
for what I have done. For as I walk, I look to You, Lord,
as my safe place of refuge. In Jesus' name, amen.

THE SUPERABUNDANTLY POWERFUL GOD

Now to Him Who, by (in consequence of) the [action of His] power that is at work within us, is able to [carry out His purpose and] do superabundantly, far over and above all that we [dare] ask or think [infinitely beyond our highest prayers, desires, thoughts, hopes, or dreams]—to Him be glory in the church and in Christ Jesus throughout all generations forever and ever. Amen (so be it).
EPHESIANS 3:20–21 AMPC

When I'm troubled, when I'm unsure of the next road I should take, when I'm fearful of the evil in this world, tell me once more, Lord, about how Your power works within me. Help me to feel Your presence within myself—my heart, mind, spirit, and soul. Remind me that it's Your energy within me that allows You to do far more than I have ever dared to ask, imagine, dream, or think. In You rests all my hope for myself, this world, and the kingdom to come. In Your name and for Your glory, both now and forever. Amen.

IN YOUR MIDST

You shall not experience or fear evil any more. . . .
Let not your hands sink down or be slow and listless.
The Lord your God is in the midst of you, a Mighty One,
a Savior [Who saves]! He will rejoice over you with joy;
He will rest [in silent satisfaction] and in His love He
will be silent and make no mention [of past sins, or even
recall them]; He will exult over you with singing.
ZEPHANIAH 3:15–17 AMPC

There are days when I just don't know what to do, Lord. I
see what's happening in this world and I'm not sure how
to respond. So I'm coming to You for comfort, guidance,
peace, and strength, Lord. Help me to rise up in Your
power. To remember that You are here, in my midst. To
rest in the knowledge that You have the power and might
not only to protect me but to make things right. And
help me to understand that no matter what mistakes I
have made in the past, You will not even mention them.

You hold all the hope, joy, peace, and courage I crave,
Lord. May I rest in Your tender calm and exultant song
in this moment. Amen.

Solace and Strength

What time I am afraid, I will have confidence in and
put my trust and reliance in You. By [the help of]
God I will praise His word; on God I lean, rely, and
confidently put my trust; I will not fear. What can man,
who is flesh, do to me? . . . For You have delivered my
life from death, yes, and my feet from falling, that I may
walk before God in the light of life and of the living.

Psalm 56:3–4, 13 ampc

When I am afraid, Lord, I turn to Your Word. There I find my solace and strength. For Your writings empower my spirit. They settle my heart so that I can breathe in Your peace.

Lord, my entire life rests upon Your Word. For on You I lean when I can't stand on my own. On You I rely when I need support. In You I can say, "Why should I be afraid? What can other humans do to me? I have the Lord. He is on my side, so I have nothing to fear."

You alone, Lord, are my confidence, both now and forever. In Jesus' name, amen.

Quietly Hoping

God's loyal love couldn't have run out, his merciful love couldn't have dried up. They're created new every morning. How great your faithfulness! I'm sticking with God (I say it over and over). He's all I've got left. God proves to be good to the man who passionately waits, to the woman who diligently seeks. It's a good thing to quietly hope, quietly hope for help from God. It's a good thing when you're young to stick it out through the hard times.

LAMENTATIONS 3:22–27 MSG

I'm so thankful Your love and mercy are new every morning, Lord. For I need a fresh supply daily. Your eternal compassion is what keeps me going; Your unstinting loving-kindness is what keeps me walking in Your light. Because You are ever faithful toward me, I can say to myself and others, "I'm sticking with God, today and every day! He will never abandon me or leave me in the dark. I hope in Him alone!"

You, Lord, have been ever so good to me because I seek You day and night. I am forever looking for Your love, guidance, and strength. I will continually and quietly hope for and expect Your help and presence every day of my life! Amen.

THE COURAGE TO STAND

*Who will rise up for me against the evildoers? Who will
stand up for me against the workers of iniquity? . . . When
I said, My foot is slipping, Your mercy and loving-kindness,
O Lord, held me up. In the multitude of my [anxious]
thoughts within me, Your comforts cheer and delight my
soul! . . . The Lord has become my High Tower and
Defense, and my God the Rock of my refuge.*

PSALM 94:16, 18–19, 22 AMPC

Some days, Lord, I feel so unprotected, alone, and helpless
against those who wish me harm that I can barely pick
my lip up off the floor. On those days, Lord, I especially
need to feel Your presence beside, behind, above, below,
and within me. When I begin slipping down into the
abyss of sadness and fear, Your mercy and love hold me
up. Your words of compassion and comfort break apart
the boulder of anxious thoughts in my head. Your words
lighten up my soul.

You alone, Lord, are my High Tower and Defense,
my Rock of refuge. In You I find the courage to stand and
the hope to strengthen my spirit. In Jesus' name, amen.

Unfathomable Love

Amid all these things we are more than conquerors
and gain a surpassing victory through Him Who loved us.
For I am persuaded beyond doubt (am sure) that neither
death nor life, nor angels nor principalities, nor things
impending and threatening nor things to come, nor powers,
nor height nor depth, nor anything else in all creation
will be able to separate us from the love of God
which is in Christ Jesus our Lord.

Romans 8:37–39 ampc

The thing that keeps me going, Lord, is Your love. That indefinable and unfathomable delight and pleasure You take in me. That's what makes me feel like I can and will do anything You ask me to do. Even more wonderful is that I can never be separated from the love You hold for me through Christ Jesus. Not even death, nor the most powerful earthly kingdom, nor angels, nor things to come, nor anything else within all that You have created can keep me from Your love.

You and Your love, Lord, are what my life, hopes, dreams, obedience, joys, and passions are all about. I am nothing without the amazing love that comes from You. In Jesus' name, amen.

A HAPPILY EVER AFTER

Mark the blameless man and behold the upright,
for there is a happy end for the man of peace. As for
transgressors, they shall be destroyed together. . . .
But the salvation of the [consistently] righteous is of
the Lord; He is their Refuge and secure Stronghold
in the time of trouble. And the Lord helps them and
delivers them; He delivers them from the wicked and
saves them, because they trust and take refuge in Him.
PSALM 37:37–40 AMPC

Sometimes being honest and good may not mean much
in this world, but I know it means a lot in Yours, Lord. For
You have promised a happily ever after for those who are
wise in Your ways and practice them no matter what the
consequences. But those who feel free to lie and cheat
will be cut off from You.

Lord, You have been and always will be my Refuge,
the one place I can run to for protection. You have been
and always will be my Stronghold when trouble comes
my way. There, abiding in Your realm of safety, I can
catch my breath, gather my wits, calm my racing heart,
and increase my strength. Amen.

ARISE!

"The LORD be with you, so that you may succeed....
You will prosper if you are careful to observe the
statutes and the rules that the LORD commanded
Moses for Israel. Be strong and courageous. Fear not;
do not be dismayed.... Arise and work! The LORD
be with you!" ... "Now set your mind and heart
to seek the LORD your God. Arise and build."

1 CHRONICLES 22:11, 13, 16, 19 ESV

Only when I am living, breathing, and working in You, Lord, do I find success. Only then can I see the way before me, the pathway You have cleared for me. Only when I follow Your commands to love You, others, and myself do I find the strength and courage to stand up for myself and those weaker than me.

So, Lord, help me put all worries aside and arise in Your name. Reveal the task You would have me perform. Show me how You would have me work in Your way. Remind me that You are with me every step, leading me, guiding me, instructing me, loving me, as I set my heart and mind to seek You, Your Word, Your will, and Your way. Amen.

The Things You Think

And now, dear brothers and sisters, one final thing.
Fix your thoughts on what is true, and honorable,
and right, and pure, and lovely, and admirable. Think
about things that are excellent and worthy of praise.
Keep putting into practice all you learned and received
from me—everything you heard from me and saw
me doing. Then the God of peace will be with you.

PHILIPPIANS 4:8–9 NLT

One of the biggest lessons I have learned from You, Father God, is that the things I think in my heart make me who I am (Proverbs 23:7). So in order to live the best life for You, I must mind my thoughts. Today and every day, Lord, help me to put my thoughts where You would have them: on things that are true, right, lovely, and good. Things that are worthy of my time and of my praise.

I am also to look continually into Your Word so I can put into practice all You have taught me. May my doing so make me more like the woman You created me to be and implant Your peace deep within me. In Jesus' name I pray, amen.

Scripture Index

OLD TESTAMENT